WHAT THE FINANCE?

REAL-WORLD FINANCIAL LITERACY SKILLS
TEENS AND YOUNG ADULTS CAN'T AFFORD
TO MISS

P. HUANG

CONTENTS

INTRODUCTION

A person either disciplines his finances or his finances discipline him.

ORRIN WOODWARD

When I was younger, I came across The Parable of the Talents in the New Testament. To say that it puzzled me greatly was an understatement. Jesus tells us the story of a master who entrusted his money to three of his servants and asked them to keep it safe for him. The first, who received five talents, invested them and returned ten in total to his master. The second, who had been given two talents, likewise invested them and brought four talents to his master. The happy master rewarded them both. The last servant buried the talent he had received and returned it to his master exactly as it had been given to him. The master was furious with this last man and told him that his talent would be taken away and given to the man who had brought back ten. The master further said, "For to everyone who has will more be given, and he will have an abundance. But from the one who has not, even what he has will be taken away" (Matthew 25: 29).

Now, this tale puzzled me. What exactly was Jesus getting at when he said that people who had more would be given more and that people who had less and refused to grow would be drained of what little they had? Wasn't this an antithesis of what spirituality itself stands for? My young mind was quite upset that Jesus seemed to be saying that the poor would be punished.

However, a few years later, the penny dropped for me when I revisited this parable. *Clink!* Jesus wasn't criticizing or belittling poor people – far from it! Instead, he was condemning the person who refused to invest and grow his talents! This revelation put a whole new twist on what I had gathered thus far. It wasn't as unfair as I had initially deemed it to be. In fact, wasn't it a very reasonable expectation?

In case you were thinking, "I wasn't expecting a Christian personal finance book," let me reassure you that this is not one. I became familiar with Bible stories because my Buddhist parents sent me to a Christian high school, so I could learn English. One New Year's Eve, I made a resolution to read some of the world's most-read books. Since I had already read Harry Potter, the next logical choice seemed to be the Bible. Full disclosure, I never finished reading the Bible, but I found some good life lessons from it. The Parable of the Talents resonates with me. I believe in living a purposeful life—developing one's "talents" and sharing them with the world.

Why This Book (Among All the Others)?

This book aims to help get you started on your financial wellness journey. It is a guide for young people who might be struggling with what to do with their own finances and want to build financial confidence and security. How do you take care of expenses and debts? How do you reconcile your income with all your growing needs? How do savings figure into all of this – especially when you are only just making ends meet? These are just a few questions that this book will attempt to answer. You might have some doubts about whether it is possible to tackle all of the above AND set aside sizable savings, which will put you in good stead for the future. I am here to tell you, *"Yes, it is possible!"*

As far as Generation Z is concerned, the following are some of the biggest challenges you are up against. These are things that the previous generations may not be able to fully help with simply because they haven't experienced the same issues.

- The job market is exceptionally competitive, especially post-pandemic.
- Expenses are skyrocketing. This includes rent, buying a car or a home, groceries, and more.
- Inflation is eating away at investments like never before. Therefore, you may not make the high returns your parents made on stocks and other securities.
- Social Security could be a thing of the past, or the benefits may be significantly reduced by the time you retire.

I'm not trying to scare you with the facts above; I understand your predicament. I have been there myself, worrying about the uncertain future and questioning if I'm managing my money correctly. The truth is everyone's personal finance journey is different, but there are some common actionable steps you can take to create financial security for yourself. In this book, I am sharing the lessons I learned from my personal finance journey, so you can make better early money decisions than me while avoiding the mistakes that I made.

This book will help you:

- Manage your income vs. expenses.
- Settle debts in the fastest and easiest manner.
- Accumulate savings for the future.
- Start investing for retirement.
- Achieve a secure financial future.

There are several books that make all the above claims. My hope is that *What the Finance* will be a gentle guide to help you take control of your finance and understand why it's never too early to get your finances in order and start investing for retirement. My own personal experience has taught me that:

1. Money does matter. It is an important tool for acquiring basic needs and improving your quality of life.
2. Money can be an excellent servant that can be trained to do your bidding.
3. Money can contribute to your overall happiness and security in life.

If you are thinking, *"Pooh! This is just a lucky person narrating her story,"* you would be wrong! Years of painstaking research, experimentation, and getting it right are at the heart of this book. It can turn your life upside down in all the right ways if you let it!

If you follow the steps this book provides, you can achieve your financial goals and find your financial happy place! Like they proverbially say, what help could be better than self-help?

Who Am I to Preach?

That's a fair question. Yours truly grew up in a middle-class family in Thailand. My parents, though exemplary at providing for all our needs and invested heavily in my education and my sisters', admittedly weren't great at managing their finances. Like many families, I grew up listening to my parents express their worries about money. All the negative money talks I heard growing up gave me a lot of anxiety about money. Seeing how financial stress can impact one's life, I aspired to be one step ahead – I wanted to manage my money well.

Early on, I realized that financial literacy is critical and that the earlier you start valuing personal finance, the better. As I grew older, this is precisely what I did – I unlearned some of the financial habits and money mindset I was taught growing up that no longer served me. Then I learned to manage my finances in a way that aligns with my values. My experience, in turn, compelled me to reach out and help others achieve financial wellness and find their financial happy place. I am not a financial expert. I am just a regular person interested in personal finance who enjoys connecting and exchanging financial knowledge and skills with others.

Over the years, I have read several finance books out there. And let me tell you – some books made me feel terrible about some of my financial decisions. Others were difficult to relate to because many of the authors were already high-income earners, making well over six figures a year. When you have a high income, it is easier to build your net worth, achieve financial independence, and reach early retirement. Not everyone will make over $100,000 a year when they are starting their career. According to Statista Research Department, in 2020, the median household income for people ages 15 to 24 was $51,645. However, if you manage your money right, you can still make the millionaire cut by your 50s or 60s, even without making a six-figure salary! The key to growing your wealth is to start early.

BUDGETING

THE FIRST STEP TO MAKING FRIENDS WITH YOUR MONEY

A budget is telling your money where to go instead of wondering where it went.

DAVE RAMSEY

As a teenager, I was given pocket money to spend on things I needed. These things are mostly school related. They could be transportation fees, books, lunch, uniforms, etc. Sometimes I would have some money left over at the end of the month. I could spend this money on things I liked. It could be anything – as long as I spent within my budget. However, my needs were few; I wasn't a kid who liked to splurge, so I put away a part of my pocket money every month, "sacrificing" things that weren't essential. One year, I decided to do without a certain brand name T-shirt that was all the rage. The following season it was out of fashion anyways, so getting it wouldn't have been worth the money. Once I got into this habit, some of the "sacrifices" no longer seemed like I was foregoing anything important at all! I discovered I could prioritize what was urgent or a necessity versus what was dictated by fads, fashion, or peer pressure.

As I got older, I also learned the art of comparative pricing – judging what I'd get by paying a certain amount and where I could get more by paying an equal or lesser amount. For instance, instead of buying a birthday card at Target for my friends, I could do the same from Dollar Tree and save a few dollars! Or better still, I could create one from materials that I already owned, such as card stock paper, glitter, and glue. Not only would my card be the only one of its kind, but it being handmade would mean more to my friends. Mind you, this was before Amazon and other online e-commerce giants. So, it did sometimes take some effort to find the item I wanted at the best price, tracing it across all the stores that sold it and then making a list of pros and cons.

One of the best tricks I learned was to buy second-hand. Often when we hear "used," it feels cheap – like you are compromising on quality. However, let me tell you that when I purchased the furniture for my apartment, I bought them from young professionals who were moving out of state. These furniture pieces were in good condition, and I got them for half the price they would have cost me. Buying pre-owned item is wallet-friendly for people who are limited on funds. It is also earth-friendly for people who are concerned about the environment. However, shopping second-hand can take time and effort, and you may not always find exactly what you want. Thus, if you have the time and don't mind doing some searching, this is a great way to save money.

Let me recount a typical scenario that most young adults seem to go through. It is the end of the month, and suddenly you realize that your car insurance premium or some other major bills are due. It had completely slipped your mind. However, when you try to settle the bill online, you find yourself short by a few hundred dollars. You scratch your head as to how this could have happened. You didn't recall making any large purchases this month, and you saved on your snack expenditure because of that new resolution to eat healthily. So how is this possible? And then it dawns on you that it was that concert you bought premium tickets for in the high of receiving your paycheck. That's where you spent your money, and now you are filled with regret. The concert could have waited, but the car insurance is due and can't be ignored without attracting a late fee if you miss the grace period. What do you do now? Call up a friend and borrow some money from them? And thus starts the slippery slope to financial misery.

Have you ever wondered exactly where all your money is going and why you are short at the end of the month? If so, this chapter is right where you should be. Let's see if we can offer you some simple budgeting hacks.

What Is a Budget?

Simply stated, a budget accounts for all your expenses against your total income. The rule of thumb that we all know but not all of us follow is that our expenses should never exceed our total income. Most people aim for a balance between income and expenditure. They are happy if they don't owe anybody money or suddenly get hit with unforeseen expenses. If you are more advanced, however, you will learn the art of saving a portion of your income every time you get it, even before you pay your bills. This concept is called "pay yourself first". You will then be able to tackle sudden expenses by using these savings.

Budgeting is the act of planning your expenses. Every month or biweekly, depending on how often your income comes in, you can decide in advance what you will spend your money on, what you can delay buying, and how much of that money can be put aside for later. The more you do this, the better you will get at tracking your expenses in advance: how much you need for snacks, new shoes, a book you've been saving up for, etc. It will also tell you where and how you can save up a bit more.

And no, I'm not a killjoy! When I suggest you should put off certain purchases or expenses, I certainly don't mean you can't have any fun. Socializing is part of growing up. When you make more new friends, you will probably go out more. This is a wonderful phase of life. If you and your friends love movies, you might spend money on movie tickets and snacks. To cut those expenses out entirely would be sad. However, you can make an arrangement with your friends. If you'd generally watch two movies a month, you could make a pact to watch one movie at the theater and one at home on your computer or TV. So, what if some of the films aren't new releases? Perhaps you could pick movies that none of you have seen, so it's still a "new" movie for everyone. Moreover, there are several streaming services available, such as Netflix, Hulu, Amazon Prime Video, Disney+, and HBO Max—each with its own exclusive content and a monthly subscription cost equivalent to or less than a movie ticket.

Why a Budget?

Let's see why budgeting is so important:

1. **It helps you sort out what is most important to you.** Would you rather have the convenience of dining out more this month or save up for a new laptop to replace your old one? How will you weigh the pros and the cons? Dining out is an immediate pleasure, whereas a new laptop could be used for years down the road. Could you manage both dining out and a new laptop if you don't go for the most expensive laptop or pick up an extra part-time job? Ultimately, the choice is all yours and depends on what you consider to be of paramount importance.

2. **Budgeting prevents overspending or, worse, falling into debt.** Not all debts are bad; however, getting into debt to live a lifestyle you cannot afford is bad debt. Bad debt does little to improve your financial circumstances, while good debt is money borrowed to build more wealth or create more income-generating assets. Have you ever been in the embarrassing position of having to borrow from a friend or your parents for something really urgent? But had you not spent on that tempting video game last month, you wouldn't have had to borrow for this emergency in the first place. Often, we also realize that what we really want now will likely be of little value in a couple of months or years. Remember that T-shirt I told you about? One of the biggest goals of budgeting is to avoid consumer debts as much as

possible and to close any you acquire as early as you can – more about this a little later.

3. **Your money habits today determine your money habits in the future.** Saving today will help you build your emergency fund for a rainy day and will help you avoid falling into debt. And for those who think working to make money is exciting, I'll tell you this – the sheen wears off. Nobody enjoys working for money forever. Focus on working smart. Develop skills to increase your income, so you can save and invest more. This way, you won't have to work all your life and might even be able to afford to take breaks in your career when needed.

4. **Emergencies are part and parcel of life.** Somebody once told me life was all about "expecting the unexpected" and I've remembered it ever since. Keeping some money aside will always help you when the tire of your new bike or car gets worn out or when you discover that something you need costs a little more than what you have – and don't even get me started on medical emergencies. Keeping savings aside for a rainy day is vital to creating a budget.

5. **Budgeting is also a great way to keep track of bad spending habits.** Say you went to Target for a bottle of shampoo. On the way to the store, you saw a sale sign in front of your favorite clothing store and decided to check it out. You found a bag that you liked and noticed that it came with a matching pair of shoes. What did you do? You bought them both. A few weeks later, your credit card bill arrived, and it dawned on you that on more than one occasion, you had purchased things you

didn't need. Do you see where I am going? Today's consumerist culture tends to push us to spend more than we need. When you learn to budget, you will learn to keep your spending habits in check. If you have it planned on paper, you are more likely to stick to your blueprint.

6. **Budgeting quells anxiety.** Suppose you are like me, somewhat of a Type A planner who worries about things that are difficult to plan for, rest assured that budgeting will allow you to sleep soundly at night. A reasonable budget accounts for routine expenses and keeps aside some extra for emergencies and the future as well. This will give you the peace of mind that you have done the best you can with the "talents" given to you.

How Do I Budget?

You may be thinking at this point, "Enough beating around the bush. I understand why budgeting helps. Just tell me how I can do this already!" If this sums up your thoughts, what comes next is exactly what you need to be reading. Here are a few tips on the hows of budgeting:

1. **What is your monthly income?** This should be easy to calculate once you tick off the sources. Do you get pocket money or an allowance? Do you make extra money via a part-time job(s)? Add up all these sources to determine your total monthly income. It is also wise to think of ways to grow your income. No matter how much you control your expenses, true financial growth will come only with increased income. With this in mind, you may want to explore having more than one

part-time job. There are a wide variety of online and offline jobs for which your skills would be ample.

2. **The 40-30-30 rule.** Some of you might have heard about the 50-30-20 rule, which suggests you keep aside 50% of your after-tax income for your needs (i.e., rent, mortgage, utility bills, essential groceries, medical bills, insurance, etc.), 30% for wants (i.e., dining, entertainment, gym membership, TV subscription, etc.), and 20% for savings or paying off debts. However, with the soaring cost of living and an unpredictable workforce, financial experts now advise tightening up your spending and moving toward the 40-30-30 rule. This is generally advised for adults once they have a regular source of income and fixed expenditures to be met. This rule requires 40% of your income to be put towards regular expenses such as rent, education, groceries, and other bills. Then, 30% of your income would be for paying off debts, loans, credit card payments, etc. And the last 30% would go into monthly savings for emergencies like medical expenses and investing for retirement. If you are saving up for an emergency fund, you can put your money in a high-yield savings or money market account, both of which will let you access them if an emergency arises. Once you have enough emergency funds to cover 3-6 months of your expenses, you can feel more secure about investing in retirement. We will cover more about investing in a later chapter.

Now, in some of your cases, you may not have too many expenses because you are still living at home or your expenses are being taken care of by your parents. This is the ideal opportunity to maximize your savings and invest. Thus, instead of the 30% mentioned above, you could aim to put 40% (or more if you can) in a high-yield savings account. Moreover, if you also don't have any debts, stay tuned because we will discuss investing your money later in the book.

3. **Categorization of expenses is an excellent way of solving the puzzle of questions like "How much?" and "For what?"** Come up with headings such as: "Groceries," "Entertainment," "Shopping," etc. These categories can then be further divided as necessary. For instance, "Shopping" could be segregated into categories such as "Necessary" and "Wish List." You can decide how much you want to spend on any one category. If you spend more on one category in certain months, you can cut back on another. For instance, if you spend a little more on shopping, you can decide to eat at home before you go out with a friend or perhaps carry homemade snacks for both of you.

4. **Track every dollar spent.** This is crucial for maintaining your budget. Always remember to write or digitally note down (in a text message, a note, an email to yourself, or in one of the many budgeting apps now available) how much you have spent and on what items. You can do this weekly if daily is too big a bug to worry about. You can round off expenses to the next dollar but keep any small change in a jar to use later. At the end of each month, convert this list of income and expenses into a spreadsheet. This is the basic concept behind a balance sheet, used by the accounting departments of large firms.

When I first started budgeting, I updated my budget spreadsheet weekly, especially the day before I receive my paycheck. Why? Well, when a lump sum falls into your bank account, wouldn't you be tempted to blow it? But – would you be as inclined to do so if you had already written a plan for it? Budgeting is a case of counting your chickens before they've hatched, I know, but it has a very positive outcome. Now that I am more familiar with my spending habits and I have automated all the payments, I only do my budget check-in once a month. I use the Mint app to track my expenses.

5. **Build an emergency savings fund.** I touched upon this in the second point and will be covering it in more detail in a later chapter. For now, just hold on to this idea.

6. **Treat saving as an expense.** When you think of saving in the future tense, you have committed your first mistake toward financial transgression. Saving should be thought of as an expense in the present tense, always! If you get $100, you should think of spending only part of it; the rest goes into savings. It is wise to set up a dedicated saving account separate from your spending account where your savings can accumulate – this way, you will be less likely to use your savings on your day-to-day expenses. Moreover, most banks give you the option to do an automatic transfer, which allows you to transfer money from your checking account to your savings account at the date or interval you choose.

7. **Review your finances monthly** – income, expenses, and savings – and look at how you fared compared to previous months. Have you spent a little more than usual? Have you saved a little more than in the last couple of months? Have you been able to cut down on some general expenses? Is your budget still aligned with your spending? These are a few questions you can ask yourself. Ideally, the spreadsheets you create for budgeting can be analyzed using pie charts, bar graphs, or charts. These will help you visualize your personal spending behavior and nip unnecessary extravagances in the bud. You can get a free sample budget sheet in the next section. If you have Microsoft Excel, you can also find a free budgeting template in the program.

8. **What are your assets?** As teenagers or young adults, you may not own a house yet. But, you may have a car for which you have to pay servicing, repairs, insurance, and gas. Create a list of other assets you own; these may include a smartphone or watch, a tablet, computer, or laptop, and a camera or other equipment you use for odd jobs. These are also items for which expenses like repair, maintenance, or replacement charges could come up. Are you expected to chip in towards any shared costs like electricity, the internet, or the TV you use at home or in your apartment? It is a good time to start thinking about these things if you haven't already.

9. **Do you have any long-term goals for your budget?** You might be planning to enroll in college, buy your first car, or go traveling. Ask yourself: "What would those costs look like?" and "How soon will I need this money?" It is always wise to set goals as early as possible. It's commonly said that the early bird catches the worm; similarly, the early planner reaps the largest benefits. In today's acronym-loving business management mantras, SMART goals are often talked about:

S – Specific: Be as clear as possible about your target. For example, "I want to create an asset base" is a vague goal. However, saying, "I will get myself a car, even a second-hand one, by the end of this year," is specific.

M – Measurable: Your goals should have a numerical component attached to them. For example, "I will save 40% of my salary this month" is better than "I will save from my salary this month."

A – Attainable: Goals must be realistic. For instance, if you don't have a job yet, saying, "I will buy a house in two years" may be too distant a dream to work towards. Set short-term goals which will help you build toward your bigger dreams.

R – Relevant: Goals must be relevant to you. It's important to understand that goal setting is a very personal activity. You must be working to make *your* dreams come true – not your parents' dreams or anyone else's. Set goals that will make a difference in your life.

T – Time-bound: Your goals must have an expiry date. Though there may be legitimate reasons why the timeframe for some goals needs to be extended, it is still a good idea to set a time by which you plan to attain them.

10. *Budgeting doesn't have to be boring; it can be fun.* If you read enough about it and come up with innovative ideas to save or invest money and treat it like a game, the tedium involved will be much less. Your purpose should be to challenge yourself to improve your financial wellness little by little. With this target in place, treat your budgeting like another video game level to cross.

Sample Budget Sheet

Here's a sample budgeting sheet you can maintain monthly. You can modify it to suit your own purposes. Add or delete rows or columns to suit your personal goals better. You can even try to apply the 40-30-30 rule mentioned earlier.

Category	Monthly Expected Amount (X)	Actual Amount (Y)	Difference (X-Y)
Income 1			
Income 2			
Income 3			
Total Income (T)			
Regular Expenses			
Rent			
Mobile Phone			
Internet			
Electricity, Water or Gas (These could come under variable too)			
Servicing or Repair of Car			
Car Insurance			
Debts (Credit cards or loan)			
Any other expenses			
Total (T1)			
Variable Expenses			
Movies			
Books			
Gifts			
Personal Grooming (shaving/ hair cut/ salon)			
Clothes			
Gas			
Food			
Other Expenses			
Total (T2)			
Expenses Total (T3=T1+T2)			
Total Savings (T-T3)			

If you want a more fancy monthly budget sheet, you can get a free one from Google Drive by following this link: tinyurl.com/mybudgetsheet, or scan the QR code below.

Key Takeaway

Budgeting is the best bet for being financially responsible. It allows you to plot your expenses vs. your income and can even take into account differences in expectations vs. reality in terms of the amount(s) you're receiving and spending. Budgeting will help you towards a secure financial future – bit by bit. Instead of saving a fixed sum for every amount, try out fun challenges for yourself, like saving a little more every month. This will keep it from getting too routine. And well, isn't this the age-old dilemma?

One of the biggest parts of budgeting is learning how to cut back on costs and expenses. Though I briefly mentioned comparing and contrasting prices and choosing pre-loved items, these are not the only ways of saving. Cutting back can be an enjoyable exercise in itself. If you are here with me thus far, on this page, come a little further, and let's look at ways in which we can reduce our cost of living and throw in a little sustainability into the bargain as well, shall we?

2

SAVING

ECONOMIZE SO YOU WON'T HAVE TO AGONIZE

Do not save what is left after spending, but spend what is left after saving.

WARREN BUFFET

Today I walked over 2 miles on foot. No, it wasn't to save gas, exactly. I could have easily taken the car to run the errands. But it was a sunny day, and the urge to walk was overpowering. Nonetheless, coming home after my refreshing walk, the thought that I had saved on fuel and possibly a parking cost was exhilarating. It seemed the best thing to have done economically, socially, and health-wise. On the way, I paused to see the changes in my locality – new buildings and shops that had come up. I even stopped to say hi to a few acquaintances. I also discovered a little café-cum-reading-corner that had never caught my eye before. These are generally the things I miss out on by zipping up and down in my car, just moving between two points, getting my work done, and coming back.

To drive home a fine point, we generally miss a lot in our mad pursuit of wanting to own things. Let me go back to the previous chapter and that brand name T-shirt I never bought. I often try to remember why I really wanted it. There wasn't exactly anything unique about it. The color wasn't one I normally picked out for myself. A lot of my wants stemmed from peer pressure. Everyone who was remotely cool seemed to own an article from that brand, and it seemed a natural feeling to want to mark my belonging with them by buying that T-shirt. However, once the fad had run its course, nobody seemed to remember that I had never owned one in the first place. Most of my friends would laugh over old photos of themselves wearing it and say things like, "Glad I outgrew that T-shirt. Such a silly thing to wear." Meanwhile, each time I heard their remarks, I would secretly congratulate myself on my prescient wisdom in never having bought it.

Saving has much to do with distinguishing between your needs and your wants. Though sometimes used interchangeably, these two words aren't the same. For example, you "need" a well-balanced meal containing the carbohydrates, proteins, vitamins, and minerals that a person of your age group and body size requires, but you may "want" a burger. Do you see the difference? Needs are the things you require for your daily life and function. Your wants stem from the desire to improve the quality of your life.

This chapter will help you focus on your needs. By no means am I saying that to want is a bad thing, either. Eventually, you can cater to your wants too. But take them one at a time and prioritize so you always have something left over to cover your overlooked needs.

Inculcating the Saving Habit

Who isn't familiar with the story of the ant and the grasshopper? Though we generally look to this story as a message about the benefits of hard work, it could just as easily be a story on savings. The grasshopper spends its summer whiling away time, singing songs and playing the guitar, while the ant consistently and meticulously collects its food and carries it back to its hill. Come winter, the tables are turned, for the ant has enough to keep itself warm, cozy, and well-fed, while the grasshopper has to seek charity for basic survival. What a severe comeuppance for such a happy little fellow who was literally mocking the ants all summer.

Most of us, including me, at times, are like the grasshopper. Made giddy on proverbs like "make hay while the sun shines" and "*carpe diem*," we often lose track of what we are working towards. It is a slow fall after that. A little at a time, we give in to small and big pleasures until reality comes calling one day. And when we are rudely awoken from our summer dreams, we realize we have burnt through our resources, with nothing to show for their loss. This section will guide you toward wise saving habits that you can acquire and implement over time.

The following is a list of some general ways to decrease your spending. From there, we will look at specific ways to cut back on your expenditure. Some of these may sound like a repetition from the previous chapter but bear with me.

1. **Record all your expenses**. I said this earlier, and I'll say it again. Step one is to always document your expenses. Without this

in place, it becomes difficult to analyze where changes in spending habits can be implemented. To do this, you can use a pen and notebook, a spreadsheet, or choose from the plethora of online apps now available such as Acorns, Mint, YNAB, etc. Once this is done, consider how you can group these expenses and calculate totals for each of them. Many of these apps have the function to view your total spending in each category every month. Check your bank account statements to ensure you have accounted for all payments.

2. **Subtract your necessary expenditure from your income to calculate your potential savings.** This is the minimum amount you want to try and put aside each month. Consider saving as part of your "expenses" and make sure to pay yourself by transferring the money into your saving account. You should also factor in other regular but not monthly expenses, like medical appointments, car insurance premiums, etc. As you earn more, you can work towards increasing your savings as a percentage of your income.

3. **Find creative ways to reduce your spending.** Spending can be reduced in many ways. I will deal with this in detail and provide a list of practical ways in which savings can become a lifestyle habit in the next section. Meanwhile, here are a few basic things to keep in mind:

- *You can search for free tools, resources, and classes instead of paying for a course.* Ditto for entertainment. There are always free community events and gatherings taking place. This is a great way of meeting people and finding free and fun entertainment.
- *Do you have Netflix, Prime, or Audible subscriptions?* Perhaps it is time to review how often you actually use them. It may be time to unsubscribe or to maintain only those that are really worth paying for.

- *Eating out versus cooking is a small lifestyle change that can make a big difference to your budget.* Don't be fooled by commercials that make cooking out to be a tedious, time-consuming, and complicated chore. If you discover the right recipes, you'll find there are many healthy, easy, and quick options to choose from.
- *Don't rush into buying things you want.* Wait and reconsider. Check out other websites and stores where the item you want is available. Oftentimes, the price of non-essential commodities like clothing, makeup, and gadgets drop within a few months of their release. You may also find huge discounts and offers during sale periods or festive occasions, like Christmas and New Year.

4. **Having a clear goal for your savings is one of the wisest moves you can make.** Don't just save for the sake of saving. Defining goals for your money will change your view of money and guide you to make decisions that improve your financial health. When I first started saving, I didn't really know why I was saving. I just knew my parents told me that saving is good. Over time I feel like all I was doing was spinning the wheeling. I ended up saving too much and didn't invest enough and make my money work for me. Now every dollar in my saving account has a clear goal. Plus, I feel less guilty when using the money in my saving account because I use them for the assigned purpose.

Here are some things to consider when financial goal setting:

- Keep your goals specific. In the previous chapter, we discussed SMART goals. Now would be a good time to recap that part.

- Your goal must be time-bound. You must have a clear idea about when (date, month, or year) you need an item and how much (the numerical sum) is required to fulfill a specific need or want (why do you need this amount?) in your life. For example, your financial goal statement should look something like: "By 20xx, I will have saved $xxxxx to take care of my _____ need(s)."

- Keep separate accounts for different goals. You will likely have more than one want or need. For instance, you could be simultaneously saving up for college and for a European tour. Keep these two savings funds separate. This will be easier for you to manage in the long run. Some saving accounts, like Wealthfront Cash Account and Ally Bank Online Savings accounts, let customers create "buckets" or "categories" to differentiate money into multiple saving goals within one account. This reduces the hassle of having to open more than one saving account for different financial goals.

- From time to time, you may have to review, modify, and change some of your goals. Your priorities will likely change over time. For instance, you may have been saving up for a vacation, but due to changes in your situation, travel may not seem as important to you now as, say, saving up for a house. That's all right as long as you review and update your finances regularly to meet your current priorities.

- Significant financial obligations can become less of a burden if you break them down. We know that work broken into smaller chunks becomes much more doable and attainable. The same goes for preparing for an exam. Constant coverage of small sections makes your final revision much easier than if you were to start studying the entire syllabus the night before the big exam. Similarly, if you need to save $5,000 in a year, you'd have to aim at saving about $417 per month, which is a little over $14 a day.

5. **Prioritizing financial needs and wants is something I'm going to keep coming back to.** For instance, if you want a new car in a couple of years, you'll have to start saving for it today. However, if you already have a car, this may not be prioritized over the savings for your college fund or your other needs. Is a new car something you need? Could this purchase be delayed? I'm not saying you can't save for a new car, but unless it is a necessity, it shouldn't take priority over your saving for educational and professional development. The skills gained from higher education and professional development will aid you in negotiating for a higher salary, which will later allow you to purchase your wants.

6. **Picking the right saving tool will depend on points 4 and 5 above.** What are your short- and long-term goals, and what is your primary priority? For short-term savings that will be used within five years, you should put money into a high-yield saving account or certificate of deposit (CD) account that is FDIC-insured. A certificate of deposit is a saving account that holds a certain amount of money for a fixed period of time, and in return, the bank pays interest on the money you deposit. If you withdraw the CD early, you could lose the interest you earn and be charged with an early withdrawal penalty. When a CD matures, and you cash it in, you will receive the original money you put in, plus the interest. FDIC stands for Federal Deposit Insurance Corporation. Per FDIC.-gov, "the FDIC is an independent agency created by the U.S. Congress to maintain stability and public confidence in the

nation's financial system". When consumers deposit money with an FDIC-insured bank, in the unlikely event of an insured-bank failure, the FDIC protects each depositor up to $250,000 per insured U.S. bank for each account ownership category.

If you are saving for the medium (six to ten years) to long term (greater than ten years), you may consider opening a brokerage account and investing your money. This is only recommended if you are seeking a higher return than the interest offered via a saving account and you can weather the volatility of the market. If you are saving for retirement, you should consider individual retirement accounts (IRAs). We will talk more about investing in the later chapter.

7. **Automated savings can make a huge difference in growing your savings.** The good thing about the times we live in is that there is very little we have to do once we put the correct technological protocol in place. It is a good idea to set up an automatic transfer, so the amount you want to be saved every month goes into your saving account as soon as you get your paycheck. This way, you won't have the chance to spend all of your earnings unless you withdraw from your savings account or break the deposit – something even the more reckless of us need to think twice about. Many direct deposit programs let you split your paycheck into multiple bank accounts. You can inquire with your company's HR regarding this.

8. **Who wouldn't love to see their money growing?** This step is the best because it entails sitting back and watching the fruits of your labor. I suggest noting your financial growth quarterly, semiannually, or at the very least, annually. This will serve as a pat on the back for the hard work and sacrifices

you've made to create your wealth base. It is also an easy way to check whether you are on track and that you are touching the expected milestones on your path. If there are any causes for concern, you can immediately address them and perhaps think of alternative ways to deposit or invest your money.

Saving Practically, Living Sustainably

"Sustainable living" seems to be the new motto these days. It refers to an overall reduction in individual or societal consumption, so the Earth's resources are conserved. It means that any production or usage is done in such a way that there is some left for future use as well. Sustainability is also a very personal choice. As a consumer, the way you use your money must ultimately align with your personal ethics. In short, sustainability is about being environmentally and socially conscious as an individual. Obviously, then, sustainability and saving go hand in hand.

Here are a few practical options you can consider in order to reduce expenses and live more sustainably. I make no claims that the following is a comprehensive list. It would be best to take stock of your daily expenses (use your budgeting sheet for this) and then come up with your own variation of where you can cut back.

1. **Make your own tea or coffee instead of buying it.** It is a small gesture towards a bigger cause. You will not just save the expense of buying something you can make but will also reduce the amount of garbage you generate by way of the Styrofoam and plastic cups you throw away each time.

2. **Walk or bike more.** Instead of using your car, you can bike and walk shorter distances or take public transportation for longer distances if you live in a city that has decent public transportation. There are so many advantages to this, along with saving on gas. It is an easy way to stay fit, and there are fewer parking hassles involved.

3. **Buying from thrift stores** sometimes finds you items that look just as expensive and are about as useful as what you get from branded stores. Taking time to check out all your options before settling on an item may help you save in a big way.

4. **Unbranded products are generally much cheaper**. Sugar, flour, canned items, and such at your local supermarket are likely to be much more affordable than the same things from a well-known brand. And what's more, they almost always taste the same.

5. **Make your own lunch.** You don't need great culinary skills to put together a sandwich or a salad. On busy days, a few eggs or maybe a piece of fruit or two can also double up as breakfast. You can also set aside a few hours on weekends to meal prep a few dishes in bulk and store them in the fridge or freezer to be used in the coming week.

6. **Use cash instead of cards.** We have entered the digital era of transactions, where most of us don't carry cash or need cash to make purchases. Though this is attractive, cash has its advantage – namely, you can't spend what you don't have. For people who tend to overspend when they go to the store, try

withdrawing a certain sum each week and leaving your cards at home when making purchases.

7. **Compare the prices of the essential services that you use.** This could include the gas, phone, internet, or electricity company you are paying for. Does it make sense to switch providers? A quick online search and getting some free quotes should give you the answers. Cable TV is also something you may want to rethink – is the time you spend watching TV worth what you pay?

8. **Drinks sap money.** If you are up for it, try cutting down on alcohol binges and nights out, then check if that saves you some money. Plus, your liver will thank you later.

9. **Keep a spare change jar.** You think loose change can't really make a difference? It can. Save all your loose change for a month and count it at the end of every month. You'll be surprised by the money you can save with such an easy tactic.

10. **Sell online.** Does your wardrobe always seem to house some items of clothing or accessories you have no idea why you bought? Why let items gather dust on your shelf when you can sell them on eBay, Facebook Marketplace, or similar sites and make some money? There are also websites and shops where you can exchange or sell old furniture, books, or other items you no longer need.

11. **Consider carpooling for regular trips, like rides to and from your office.** This is a great way of saving on fuel. Perhaps you'll also make a like-minded friend along the way.

12. **Don't overdraft.** Being eligible for large overdrafts does make your spending power seem more lavish. However, on average, banks make over one billion dollars from overdraft fees annually. These fees can dig you deeper into debt. When you learn to budget properly, you will be more cautious about your spending habits, and an overdraft should slowly become a thing of the past.

13. **Insurance is a necessary financial tool to secure your future.** However, there may be better deals that offer the same coverage for lower premiums. Be sure to do your homework before choosing your policy. Last year, I got a new quote for my car insurance from the same provider, and I was able to save $110 on the same policy.

14. **Payday loans look very tempting; however, they come with big risks.** Some online loans are outright scams to cheat people out of their money. Never risk your money or your peace of mind by taking on one of these.

15. **Clean everything at home.** You can get a dry-cleaning kit for your clothes instead of incurring the service charges of a dry cleaner. And did you know that everyday products like baking soda, lime, and toothpaste can be used to clean stains and spills? These can be just as effective as the branded sprays and cleaners you get from the store.

16. **Handmade and personalized gifts and cards are a great way to show your love, affection, and appreciation for people.** You will, of course, spend some money on the raw materials and some time and energy putting them

together. But it is worth the effort when you realize that store-bought items generally cost more than double and perhaps mean less to the person receiving them.

17. **You don't need a gym membership to stay fit.** You can walk, bike, stretch, swim or dance away your excess calories at no cost. There are a plethora of YouTube and Instagram channels you can follow to find an exercise regimen you are interested in. However, if you are a regular gym goer and enjoy using gym equipment, like myself, don't hesitate to get a gym membership. Regular exercise improves overall health and reduces the risks of various diseases.

18. **Personal grooming is another area where you can save some money.** All right, perhaps you will still need a haircut, but your eyebrows, shaves, manicures, and pedicures can all be done at home. All you need is to set some time aside for yourself.

19. **Turning off lights and using energy-saving bulbs can go a long way in saving electricity consumption.** Similarly, getting electronic items like your fridge and washing machine serviced periodically is not an expense but a way to ensure they consume less power. This will, in turn, save you money.

20. **Dental hygiene seems rather out of place in a list of how to save money.** But believe me, brushing and flossing your teeth daily saves you the expense and misery of procedures like root canals, extractions, bonding, and dentures.

These are just a few ideas. However, you can easily find plenty of other options to help you cut down on immediate and future expenses. If saving becomes a habit, it can change your life for the better.

Sample Sheet for Cutting Expenses

Here's a sample sheet you can use to figure out where you can cut back on expenses. You can modify the list provided to suit your particular needs. Most of the items here you should have taken into account on your budget sheet. There may also be some items on your list for which cutting costs is impossible, such as rent. Against those particular items, column Y will show $0.

Categories	Monthly Expense (X)	Amount that can be saved (Y)	New monthly expense (X-Y)
Regular Expenses			
Rent			
Mobile Phone			
Internet			
Electricity, Water or Gas (These could come under variable too)			
Servicing or Repair of Car			
Car Insurance			
Debts (Credit cards or loan)			
Other expenses			
Total (T1)			
Variable Expenses			
Movies			
Books			
Gifts			
Personal Grooming (shaving/ hair cut/ salon)			
Clothes			
Gas			
Food			
Other Expenses			
Total (T2)			
Expenses Total (T3=T1+T2)			

For people who love a little challenge, below is the 52- week saving challenge to kickstart your first $5,000 emergency fund or saving for any big purchases. You can double the deposit amount to make it a $10,000 saving challenge if you want to turn it up a notch.

Week	Deposit	Balance	Complete ✓
1	$25	$25	
2	$35	$60	
3	$40	$100	
4	$50	$150	
5	$55	$205	
6	$60	$265	
7	$65	$330	
8	$70	$400	
9	$75	$475	
10	$80	$555	
11	$85	$640	
12	$90	$730	
13	$95	$825	
14	$100	$925	
15	$105	$1,030	
16	$110	$1,140	
17	$115	$1,255	
18	$120	$1,375	
19	$125	$1,500	
20	$130	$1,630	
21	$135	$1,765	
22	$140	$1,905	
23	$145	$2,050	
24	$150	$2,200	
25	$150	$2,350	
26	$150	$2,500	

Week	Deposit	Balance	Complete ✓
27	$150	$150	
28	$150	$300	
29	$150	$450	
30	$145	$595	
31	$140	$735	
32	$135	$870	
33	$130	$1,000	
34	$125	$1,125	
35	$120	$1,245	
36	$115	$1,360	
37	$110	$1,470	
38	$105	$1,575	
39	$100	$1,675	
40	$95	$1,770	
41	$90	$1,860	
42	$85	$1,945	
43	$80	$2,025	
44	$75	$2,100	
45	$70	$2,170	
46	$65	$2,235	
47	$60	$2,295	
48	$55	$2,350	
49	$50	$2,400	
50	$45	$2,445	
51	$30	$2,475	
52	$25	$2,500	

Key Takeaway

This chapter, I hope, has been instrumental in providing you with several ideas on how the idea of savings can be turned into a reality. I discussed many general techniques to save money and then moved on to very specific ways in which you could turn your lifestyle around, including sustainability. It is not just about the money you save; it is also about doing your bit for the environment and the society around you. When cultivated over time, these habits will help you save more for your visible and invisible future needs.

Savings is an essential part of financial management because it not only helps you grow monetarily but also helps in remaining debt-free as well. The next chapter will tell you all you need to know about debts – how not to get into the bad ones, how to get rid of them, and how to manage them in case you have running loans.

3

DEBT

BORROWED MONEY CAN BE A LOT MORE EXPENSIVE THAN YOU THINK

Some debts are fun when you are acquiring them, but none are fun when you set about retiring them.

OGDEN NASH

J ust a day or two ago, I was browsing the internet, and I came across the story of a father who took out loans for his son to pursue a college education. The father was 57 and a photographer with an annual income of around $40,000. He took out a PLUS loan, a federal loan to pay the fees, and a year later found he had acquired a colossal debt. He says that the whole process was so disarmingly simple, taking just a little over a minute to complete online. His sole focus was to provide the best he could for his son, so he did not bother with the finer details. However, now the father finds himself in the position of having to pay $760.00 a month until the age of 88 in order to settle this debt of $104,118. It is not an impossible figure, but one which will be hard to manage once he retires from work soon. In retrospect, he feels that the amount should not have been so easy to borrow (Sheffey, 2021).

This is just one instance of how normal, everyday, and otherwise diligent people can easily be enticed into the debt trap. The sad part is that this trap is easy to get into and not so easy to get out of. However, let us not get side-tracked and leave the stories of the U.S. student debt crisis and predatory lending for another day. For those of you who have outstanding loans and other sums, paying these off must be a priority in your budget. If you have high-interest debt–anything above a 7% interest rate, I strongly suggest you clear this debt as soon as possible. Easier said than done, you say? It can be accomplished, I assure you.

How to Be Debt-Free in Your 30s

Late 20s and early 30s are ridden with emotional and physical turmoil. Physically, some of you will find yourselves slowing down. You will perhaps find yourselves wanting to take things slower. The work-hard-party-hard lifestyle that was your life in your early and mid-20s may not exactly be viable now.

Perhaps add to the "adulting" list are other new commitments and responsibilities – engagement, marriage, kids, a new home, and/or a car. The list can seem never-ending. This is certainly not the time you want to be riddled with the "sins of your past" and debts you incurred in fits of lavishness. But if you currently have a loan running, do not fret. About 340 million people in the U.S. have debts. You are not alone. Let me tell you what you can do to save yourself a load of headaches in the coming decade:

1. **Know that you are not alone.** Having debts can be a shameful, embarrassing experience. The hopelessness people feel about their financial circumstances can cause them to avoid facing it altogether, thus escalating their money problems. The first step in dealing with debt is to face it head-on and seek people you can speak with truthfully and openly about your situation. I understand no one wants to admit that their finances are spiraling out of control. However, there are several online communities where asking money questions is not only a norm, but it's also encouraged. Plus, you can also post anonymously. Please remember, as you go through your debt repayment journey, you are NOT your debt. You are NOT broken. You are NOT a bad person for having debt. You just didn't know better when you made the financial decision you made. It's okay to feel overwhelmed about not having your finance all together at the moment, but trust me, it's not too late for you to take action today to create a better financial future in the months and years to come. The fact that you are reading this book already shows that you are one step closer to improving your financial health.

2. **It is okay to feel overwhelmed and deeply frustrated** when you are trying to tackle several outstanding amounts simultaneously. One easy method of repaying debts is the snowball method, suggested by Dave Ramsey. Create a list of your loans from smallest to largest. Then focus on paying the smallest balance first and keep paying the minimum payable amount on all. other loans. Once your smallest loan is repaid, refocus on the next smallest loan, and so on, until you have settled all of them. The

key is to remain focused and not add to the existing burden. Research suggests that seeing your loans disappear has such a motivating effect that people are encouraged to keep trying until they are debt free.

3. **Engaging damage control by not taking on new loans is vital.** This would simply replace one devil with another, and you will never get out of the hole. You must analyze what makes you spend. Ditching your credit card will help prevent you from adding to your debts. Perhaps you could try not visiting your favorite store(s), where you easily succumb to the latest marketing gimmicks. The trick can be summed up in two words and one term: self-control. If you are wondering whether you are taking on too much debt, a general rule of thumb is to keep your debt-to-income ratio below 40%. To calculate your debt-to-income ratio, you will first add up all your debts. This includes your monthly payments for rent or mortgage, auto loans, student loans, and credit card payments. Next, determine your gross monthly income (your income before tax). Then, divide your debts by your gross monthly income and multiply by 100, and you will have your debt-to-income ratio.

4. **Start your emergency fund**. When you already have loans running, an emergency fund doesn't sound sensible, right? Who wants to put aside money when you are focusing on clearing away existing loans? Logically, it would seem a better bet to forget saving now and simply use every cent available to clear away your debt; however, this would be a mistake. When you have no cash for emergencies, the whole process of repaying debts can seem disheartening, and people often turn back to the debt-making process to take

care of these emergencies. Hence, put away an emergency fund first and then work on tackling the loans – more on this shortly.

5. **Many people make the mistake of biting off more than they can chew.** Thus, even before they are debt free, they try to improve their lifestyle by getting bigger homes, fancier cars, more stylish (aka more expensive) clothes, and so on. Peer and collective pressure to measure up to certain standards is often the motive behind this. However, maintaining a simple lifestyle and living below your means can help you clear your debts faster. We will deal with how to avoid an expansionist lifestyle a little later in this chapter.

6. **Increase your income.** There is only so much you can do to keep your expenses curbed, and inflation will see to it that even basic expenses go up while your income does not grow at the same rate. So, does this mean you are predestined for doom? Not at all. It's commonly said that "when the going gets tough, the tough get going," and I agree. There are multiple side gigs and avenues available today that can make a fast buck without compromising your existing income(s). The truth is there is a limit to how much you can cut on your expenses, but there is no limit to how much you can earn. All you need to do is find your strengths and suitable opportunities to maximize and monetize. Pick up a side hustle and negotiate your salary to make sure you don't leave money on the table. In the coming sections, I will provide you with some side hustles that you can explore.

7. **Know your priority.** This has been mentioned in every chapter thus far, but it's worth mentioning again – prioritize your needs and cut back on unnecessary things. Developing this habit will be vital as you move ahead. Use some of the 20 practical tips listed in the previous chapter to save you some solid money.

Building an Emergency Fund

Emergency funds are savings accounts you set aside for specific needs. They will depend on what constitutes an emergency for you. For instance, you might have a dedicated account for all expenses related to your health, such as routine dental and eye checkups. You can also set up an account merely to take care of expenses when or if you are in between jobs. The uses you ascribe to your emergency fund are entirely based on your personal choice.

At least some of us would have had a favorite blanket as a child. Think about those days when you couldn't find it – the anxiety and meltdowns that were caused by it being put in the wash by your parents. An emergency fund is the adult version of your favorite blanket. It offers the same safety and comfort that you derived from your blanket as a child. An emergency fund is your first defense against an unexpected bill that could lead you to take out a high-interest loan and fall into a debt trap.

Financial experts advise you to save up at least three to six months' worth of expenses in an emergency fund.

You can build an emergency fund in three steps:

1. Set a realistic target for the emergency fund based on your budget sheet. Imagine if you were out of work without an income. What would your living expenses

be? Slowly work towards putting this figure into your emergency savings fund.

2. High-yield saving accounts (HYSA) can help you reach this target faster. If you keep your saving in a regular checking account, it can be pretty tempting to withdraw from it for personal use, and you won't earn any interest on your deposit. Some banks also require a minimum deposit and charge maintenance fees. So, do your homework. Find an account with minimal or no fees that give you a reasonable interest rate. This will help you grow your monetary base and reduce some losses due to inflation. Personally, I have my saving with Wealthfront and am getting 3.30% APY (as of November 2022).

3. Automate your deposits into your emergency fund monthly or biweekly. Automating the process will ensure you don't have to remind yourself every month.

Avoiding Lifestyle Inflation

With every pay hike and increment, your lifestyle has a tendency to change from one that started out as frugal to one that is more lavish. You must have noticed this in people around you, if not in yourself. You may decide to upgrade your vehicle to a luxury car or turn a luxury self-care service into a weekly routine. A one-bedroom apartment is replaced by a two-bedroom or a bigger home. The way you dress becomes more sophisticated over time. Even your eating habits aren't entirely free of this inflation. Sometimes these changes aren't as much need-based as they are want-based. Often it is more about projecting an outward appearance of the prosperity you are catching up with. Is there anything wrong with this? Definitely not! Who among us wouldn't want to treat ourselves and cushion our lives further?

The problem, though, is when this lifestyle inflation gets out of hand and curbs the savings we could be making. The money we splurge on dining at fancy restaurants and on expensive clothes is money we could be investing and putting toward other needs and emergencies that could arise in the near future.

It may not be strictly possible to keep your spending the same over the years, but by trying to reduce the disparity between your spending levels over the years, you can actually make a huge difference in attaining your financial goals faster and with less hassle. Let's look at a few ways this can be done:

1. **Determine your long-term goals.** For instance, maybe you would like to work for a while before starting your own venture. Maybe you plan to travel throughout your life and visit many countries. Perhaps you want to make enough of an asset base to be able to live off it completely. Whatever your ultimate objectives are, you can work backward and develop short-term steps to achieve them.

2. **Pay off your unsecured loans first** because they are the worst wealth inhibitors. Unsecured loans can be any one or a combination of credit card payments, student loans, or personal loans. Never expand your lifestyle majorly until you get rid of all these loans, big and small. Otherwise, you will find yourself in the same rut of making and repaying money your entire life.

3. **Live below your means.** Structural expenses in America (i.e., housing and transportation) are quite

high. Many Americans struggle all their lives paying them off. Before getting yourself into a home or car loan, weigh all your options carefully. How will you afford these payments if you are out of a job for a while? Could you perhaps look at a smaller house or a less expensive car? These are some questions to ask yourself before jumping into action.

4. **Automation of savings is highly useful** and has been touched upon several times previously. I'll refrain from elaborating on it further here.

5. **Use your credit card wisely.** As I have mentioned before, one of the worst things for a spend-thrift to own is a credit card. It tempts you to spend money that you don't yet have. If you know you're an unreliable spender susceptible to the charms of shopping, restrict the use of your credit card to only small purchases, like gas or utility bills. That way, you can still build your credit and minimize your risks of overspending.

6. **As you invest more, you earn more.** This is called a passive income, i.e., an income you don't need to actively work for. As you earn this, a part of you won't be able to resist spending it. Curb this urge by reinvesting your passive income. You can explore new options of investing, of course, but don't let earnings from your passive income sit too long in your regular checking account, where there is always the danger of it being used up on some mundane expense.

7. **Build "stealth wealth"** rather than flaunting your status by owning or updating your gadgets yearly to the latest and most expensive smartphone, etc. The more you spend on these external trappings, the less

you will have to invest, meaning you will have less money that can be left to grow on its own. Aim for a simple lifestyle that will let you put the bulk of your earnings into savings and investments.

8. **Pick like-minded friends and social gatherings that align with and support your financial goals.** When you have friends who, like you, are working hard towards financial stability, you will not feel the pressure to keep up appearances. Not only will you find genuine people who will be true friends, but you'll also save money by not being in the rat race and spending more to flaunt your "status." Instead of going to upscale joints where you will inevitably end up paying more for food and drinks, have small get-togethers at one of your homes. If you decide on homemade snacks or meals, you can reduce the expenditure on food and drinks.

9. **Keep an eye on your percentages.** Set a percentage for an increase in your spending budget when your income increases. As I mentioned earlier, sometimes it is simply not possible to live as frugally as you did in your teens. For example, perhaps you can't fathom the idea of returning to shared accommodation, even though it would save a bit on your rental expense. However, you can look at the percentage increase in your income and then fix a certain percentage increase on your expenditure as well. Anything above that limit should be curtailed or stopped. You must also consider the tax rates on your higher income before you set the limit on your expenditure amount. For example, if your income has increased by $1,500 every month, the amount you

actually receive in hand may only be $1,000 after tax. So, if you think of spending a third of this, the amount would be about $333, not the $500 you would expect.

Side Hustles and Gigs

Side hustles and gigs are basically jobs that can supplement your income. Obviously, since these cannot happen within your regular work hours, these options have to involve flexible timing and space. Side hustles will provide you with a supplemental income that the hikes or increments of your regular job may not be able to offer, and these can greatly help you ease your financial burdens. This is why, financially speaking, it makes much sense to check out these options. However, a word of caution I would add here is not to overdo them to the point that you get side-tracked from schoolwork or your regular job. Any side hustle or gig must still give you the time to rest, eat, and take care of your health.

Let us look at some avenues that could help you make as much as $1,000 per month over and above your regular income:

1. **Drop-shipping** is a marketing model where you act as an intermediary between the supplier and the customer. You market products, items, or services the supplier provides via your website or the supplier's web portal. For every sales request and payment you make, you will receive a percentage of the price the customer pays. This is quite an easy way of making money. You may have to narrow it down to items or products that are easy to market.

2. **Running a wholesale business** is when you buy products or items from the manufacturer or supplier in bulk at wholesale prices, then sell them to individual customers. To start this business, you will need money to buy the items and perhaps even the space to stock them. However, many suppliers will give you credit lines, enabling you to pay for your purchases later once you've started getting steady income from your customers.

3. **Freelancing gigs** can earn you some money on the side. Depending on your skill, you could freelance as a writer, illustrator, narrator, and so on. Dedicated sites such as Upwork or Fiverr help you create profiles where you can sell your work or skills to potential clients. The only flipside to this is that this may take some time to build up your portfolio and get regular customers.

4. **Blogging** is another great way to make some money on the side. It involves an investment in a laptop and perhaps a fast internet service for your research, but otherwise it won't cost much to set up. You could start off with a personal blogging site that doubles as a portfolio of work for interested clients. If you are one of the lucky ones whose blog catches on and goes viral, you could make steady revenue with each new post. Otherwise, you can create profiles on various platforms to woo potential clients with your work experience and writing samples.

5. **Affiliate marketing** involves tying yourself up with a company, or a particular product line of a company, then marketing those products. It may take you some time to grasp the tricks of the trade. However, if you can find an able mentor who can

guide you through the process, you may find the results are well worth the effort.

6. **Sell your art.** If you are artistic and want to both promote your art in the world and make some money from it, consider investing in a print-on-demand store. Print-on-demand stores print a particular design or artwork of your making onto products like T-shirts, mugs, or other objects and then ship them to the customer.

7. **Creating and selling information products like courses or eBooks** is a great way of earning a passive income. Each time somebody buys your book or resource, you earn money. You will have to narrow down to a niche area that people may have trouble with and invest some time and energy in marketing your content.

8. **Becoming a social influencer** is the new type of hustle everyone is talking about. If you are a good narrator and can quickly and easily produce engaging videos and content, then this is what you should be looking at. Instagram and YouTube provide many incentives to people who can garner followers. You can also develop sponsored content for specific products in order to earn more.

9. **Virtual assistance** sounds very new-fangled – almost like Jarvis from *Iron Man* – but this is a far easier concept in reality. Virtual assistants are hired to do all the work that a secretary or a personal assistant would do in the office, such as setting up calls, arranging virtual meetings, preparing reports, and researching projects or partnerships. They can also do social media or take on part of the PR role within an

organization. The only difference is that virtual assistants have the flexibility of working from home or from any other remote location.

10. **Photography** is a skill that can earn you a bit of money. There are websites that either buy photos captured by you or upload them for you so that each time somebody buys them off the site, you earn a royalty on your work.

11. **Become a rideshare or delivery driver.** If you own a car, you can make money driving people around or delivering groceries and food. If you don't mind meeting new strangers and driving them to different locations, you can become a driver for Uber and Lyft. If you prefer delivering groceries and food, Instacart, DoorDash, Grubhub, Postmates, Shipt, and Uber Eats are good options. If you are a handy person and good at running errands, you can check out TaskRabbit.

Paying Off Debts When Broke

Supposing you are so deep in a financial hole that redemption seems impossible, what do you do then? Here is my advice for keeping it together and repaying the loan:

1. Create a budget that makes paying off your loans your top priority. Work out when you can potentially be debt free, at a rate you can realistically pay off the installments.

2. Differentiate between broke and overspent – the two aren't the same. If you really have no money at all, you are broke. Otherwise, you can make a few changes in

your lifestyle and allocate your budget to start paying off your dues.

3. Decide how you want to tackle your loans – smallest to biggest or vice versa. The strategies listed in the next section will give you some guidelines on how to tackle your debts.

4. Reduce expenses by doing away with things that can be bought later and focusing only on essentials like housing, food, basic clothing, and transportation.

5. Look at alternative sources for earning an additional income or two. Use the list in the previous section for inspiration.

6. Don't take on more liability than you already have, and ensure that, until all your debts are repaid, you don't apply for more loans.

7. Ask your creditors if they are willing to settle for a lower interest rate so you can make payments faster.

8. Pay installments on time to avoid incurring fines, thereby increasing your loan burden.

9. Consumer credit counseling agencies work with debtors to help them pay off outstanding amounts. A credit counselor can help you create a customized debt management plan.

10. Take it bit by bit. As we know, Rome wasn't built in a day. Work steadily and consistently at your plan, and you will get there. Don't look at the total debt and get dispirited.

Mistakes to Avoid While Paying off Loans

This section is basically a list of don'ts when it comes to dealing with the repayment of debts. Here are some things you should stop yourself from doing:

1. Maintaining the same old overspending habits.
2. Trying to cope with the debt all on your own, without professional advice.
3. Consulting scam debt managers who will claim unrealistic results towards the clearing of your debts and charge you hefty consulting fees or charges.
4. Creating an impractical budget that doesn't factor in your essential needs and requirements.
5. Trying to pay off several debts at once can quickly become overwhelming and disheartening. Instead, focus on clearing one debt at a time without delaying the minimum payments on any of your loan amounts.
6. Closing credit cards once you have paid off the bills. Instead, keep the card active. Doing this helps lengthen your credit history and build your credit score. Using only a small portion of the credit available to you will earn you many rewards and bonus points as well. So, it makes sense to keep the card unless the service charges on it are uncomfortably high.
7. Using money from your 401(k) retirement fund to pay off debts. Instead, leave your retirement fund untouched because you don't want to be working all your life. There are also penalties for breaking this fund early.
8. Failing to create an emergency fund.
9. Not verifying your credit report. Always verify your credit reports because there may be errors, and you could end up paying unnecessarily for a mistake. Be sure to check for incorrect delinquencies and balances that could hurt your credit score.
10. Not prioritizing your loans.

11. Not transferring credits to other cards with lower interest rates. Instead, apply for a balance transfer credit card on which the interest rate is lower or 0%. This will help you settle outstanding amounts faster by paying smaller amounts. However, remember that these are introductory rates, and the interest rate will surge upward after the promotional period. These cards are to be used for interim relief only.

Strategies to Clear Debts

This section is slightly more technical and provides you with options to pay off your loans. Remember, before you adopt any method, it is best to consider your personal situation. Listed below are four common methods of debt clearing:

Debt Snowball	**Debt Avalanche**
• Your spare money goes towards clearing the smallest debt first, then the next smallest, and so on. • It works psychologically well because people remain motivated seeing their debts disappear one by one.	• Your spare money goes towards clearing the debt with the largest interest rate. • Financially it works better because it would save you money on interest compared to the snowball method.
Debt Consolidation	**Debt Management**
• Combining all your debts into one large debt so that there is only one monthly payment to make. • This is easier than keeping track of several loans.	• You work with a credit counseling agency who will correspond with each of your creditors and arrange a payment plan that suits you. • Having to make only one payment simplifies your task.

Let me also list a few options available to you while clearing your debts:

1. **Balance Transfer:** As mentioned above, you can apply for a balance transfer card where one or several of your loans can be transferred for a specified amount of time to a 0% interest rate credit card. This would allow you some breathing space in paying off those debts.

2. **Personal Loan:** In some cases, depending on your credit score, you can get a personal loan on which the interest could be lower than the ones you are currently paying off. This loan can be used to settle your existing loans, and then you would have only payment and probably at a lower interest rate to settle.

3. **Debt settlement:** You or one of your friends or family can bargain with the creditors to settle a debt for less than what is outstanding. If they accept, for example, a loan with a balance of $3,000, it could potentially be settled at $2,000. But for this to happen, the creditor's consent is mandatory.

4. **Bankruptcy:** You can file for bankruptcy in two ways. In the first kind (called 'Chapter 7 bankruptcy') you will be obliged to sell all your assets and pay off your creditors. The second kind (called 'Chapter 13 bankruptcy') will let you set up a payment plan for three-five years, which you must meet, and then be discharged from further obligations after that period. Keep in mind that filing for bankruptcy should be a last resort because it will negatively impact your credit score for several years to come.

Student Loan Refinancing

Student loan refinancing is gathering some or all of your loans into one single loan at a lower interest rate so that you can clear your debt faster. This is a good solution if you have several loans running and can also be used for just one loan.

Though conceptually similar, student loan refinancing refers to the options available through private channels, like banks and other student loan lenders, while student loan consolidation is the government or federal scheme. One major difference between the two is that student loan consolidation need not give you a lower interest rate on a loan. Whereas the main objective of loan refinancing is consolidating your loans, then obtaining a new term period and lower interest rate.

Below is a computation chart of how student loan refinancing can help:

A lower interest rate means you save monthly, and on total interest paid.		
Original loan	Refinanced loan at lower interest rate	**Difference** (Variable depending on the amount of the original loan and interest vs. the refinanced loan and a renegotiated interest percentage.)
$30,000 10-year term 7.5% interest	$ 30,000 10-year term 5.5% interest	
Approximate monthly payment: $356.11	Approximate monthly payment: $325.58	You save $30.53 monthly.
Approximate total interest: $12,732.64	Approximate total interest: $9,069.46	You save $3,663.18 on total interest paid.
A shorter repayment term will save on the total interest paid.		
Original loan	Refinanced loan at shorter term	Difference
$30,000 10-year term 7.5% interest	$ 30,000 5-year term 7.5% interest	
Approximate monthly payment: $356.11	Approximate monthly payment: $601.14	You spend $245.03 more monthly.
Approximate total interest: $12,732.64	Approximate total interest: $6,068.31	You save $6,664.33 on total interest paid.
The lower interest rate and shorter repayment term means you'll save on total interest paid.		
Original loan	Refinanced loan at lower interest and shorter term	Difference
$30,000 10-year term 7.5% interest	$30,000 5-year term 5.5% interest	
Approximate monthly payment: $356.11	Approximate monthly payment: $573.03	You spend $216.92 more monthly.
Approximate total interest: $12,732.64	Approximate total interest: $4,382.09	You save $8,349.91 on total interest paid.
A longer repayment term will allow you to save on the monthly amounts paid.		
Original loan	Refinanced loan at longer term	Difference
$30,000 10-year term 7.5% interest	$30,000 15-year term 7.5% interest	
Approximate monthly payment: $356.11	Approximate monthly payment: $278.10	You save $78.01 monthly.
Approximate total interest: $12,732.64	Approximate total interest: $20,058.67	You spend $7,326.03 more on the total interest paid.

These are some more points to consider when applying for student loan refinancing:

1. Drawbacks: Refinancing is a great option to lower your monthly loan burden or your overall loan burden. However, federal loans have many benefits in terms of repayment and are sometimes even waived. These options are not available on refinanced loans. If you refinance some of your federal loans, you will lose out on these benefits. Refinancing your student loans with private lenders will make you ineligible now and later for all federal loan forgiveness programs.

2. Your credit score will not be impacted much whether you decide to refinance your student loans or not. Multiple loans open with multiple lenders are usually worse for your credit score than refinancing your student loan.

3. Student loan lenders will look at your credit score, debt history, and income to check whether you are eligible for refinancing your student loan.

4. While deciding how to refinance your student loans, you must keep your goal clear: Do you want to lower your monthly and overall burden? Do you want to reduce only your monthly burden for now? Do you want to lower your overall burden but can pay a little more monthly?

5. What are your existing loans – are they mostly private? If you have federal loans, does it make sense to waive the benefits you may get on them?

6. What are the customer support services you would want from your lender? Is the lender reputable and reliable?

Key Takeaway

As you would have observed by now, one of the best things about remaining debt-free or paying loans on time is that you can maintain a good credit score. If you want to learn more about credit scores and how you can maintain a good score, let's proceed to the next chapter.

4

CREDIT SCORE

YOUR CREDIBILITY IN THE WORLD OF PERSONAL FINANCE

If you don't take good care of your credit, then your credit won't take good care of you.

TYLER GREGORY

E thics and reputation matter in one's professional life as much as in one's personal life. The one is inextricably bound to the other. Let me ask you a hypothetical question. Suppose two people ask you for small loans of $200 and $100, respectively. The first is a hardworking, sincere person whom you know personally as very honest, with no history of ever cheating anyone. Known to be very scrupulous about using money only for needs, this person approaches you with claims of having lost their wallet and wanting the sum above for an emergency and tells you clearly when they would be able to return the amount to you. The second is a person who is known to throw money about and partake in lavish parties and is known as a serial borrower with a history of loans from several people to whom they have as yet not returned the sums. This second person asks you for a smaller amount, which they also claim is towards meeting an emergency. Assuming you have about $350 to spare at this particular time, whom would you be more likely to lend your money to, and why?

Most of you would be spot on in your assessment that lending to the first person would be a safer bet. Not only is this a good person to have on your side, but if you were to run into difficulties, later on, you can be assured that they will return your amount as soon as it is possible for them to do it. The bad reputation of the second person precedes them, and you should most likely make an excuse as to why you can't lend them the amount they are asking for. You would be worried, and rightly so, that this person will take your money and that you will not hear from them again.

A credit score is basically your reputation when it comes to your creditworthiness. Taking into consideration a variety of parameters, this score computes how safe you are as a borrower. The better your score or reputation, the easier it will be for you to apply and get accepted for various loans and other financial benefits.

This section will aim to answer questions like what a credit score is, why it is important to maintain a good score, how a credit score differs from a credit report, and how you can maintain a good credit score so that you can avail yourself of the best financial propositions available.

What Is Credit?

Credit is a loaded word that has many implications. Let me start by telling you what credit is not. Credit is not, as popularly misunderstood, the money given to you free of cost. Credit is a sum of money allocated for your use, with the intent that you repay it with interest over time.

When lenders decide whether or not to give you credit, the amount, the interest rate, and the term of the loan are all decided based on your credit history. Your credit history is whether you have taken loans earlier and how efficient you were in repaying them. Based on various factors (which I will be coming to in a bit), your credit score is the summary of how good a borrower you are. The higher your credit score, the better or safer you are considered by lenders, and the easier it will be for you to get loans approved.

A credit report sounds synonymous with a credit score, but the two terms aren't the same.

Credit Score	Credit Report
1. A credit score is a glimpse of your credit history at a particular point of time. 2. This is measured by something called the FICO (Fair Isaac Corporation) score, which is a value between 300 and 850. 3. FICO Score takes into account: your repayment history, the loan amount outstanding in your name, the length of your credit history, your credit mix, and any new credit requests made by you.	1. A credit report is a document that offers information on the history of your credit use. Depending on the information, it may cover information over the past 7-10 years. 2. Credit reports are monitored by 3 consumer credit reporting agencies: Equifax, Experian, and Transunion 3. The report will include information on any company that extended you loans, current loans against your name, your repayment history, and bankruptcies, if any.

You can download your credit report from any of the three consumer credit reporting agencies once a year, free of cost. It is good to check your record every year and clear up any mistakes in them.

Let us now look at what exactly a credit score is and how it is computed.

Credit or FICO Score

Your FICO score is a value between 300 (poor) to 850 (best) based on the following:

1. *Payment History* (35%): The score takes into account how many times you have made your payments on time, paid them late, or missed them entirely. Obviously, the score is higher for people who have made their payments on time. If you miss your payments or delay them, then your score will drop.
2. *Credit utilization* (30%): the FICO score looks at any outstanding balances that you owe on loans that you have taken. It also looks at your credit card payments and the percentage of credit you have utilized. This score is better for people who keep their credit utilization below 30% of their credit limit.
3. *Credit History Length* (15%): The longer you have had a healthy credit history, the better your score will be. This means having a credit card and utilizing it within the credit limits will perhaps give you a better score than not owning a credit card at all.
4. *New Credit* (10%): If you have had several open loans in the recent past, it may affect your FICO score negatively and bring it down.

5. *Types of Credit* (10%): A mix of the types of credit, like installment and revolving, will be better than having just one kind of credit type.

You must also remember that the FICO score gives a weighted advantage to some factors more than others. The percentages I have put in brackets above will provide you with an idea about which factors are most important to your score. For instance, payment history is given maximum weightage, while new credit and credit mix are given the least.

Types of Credit Available

There are several types of credit available to customers based on the terms of repayment and the nature of the credit line.

Installment loans are loans you take out for a certain sum and then repay over a particular timeframe with interest, such as student loans. Going back to the example I used in the previous chapter, suppose you take out a student loan toward fulfilling your tuition at college for $30,000 at 7.5 % interest for a period of 10 years. At the above interest rate, you will pay $356.11 monthly for ten years to close and settle this loan. In total, you will be paying $30,000 toward the principal and $12,732.64 toward the interest. Auto loans and mortgages are also considered installment loans. You make a down payment against the total price of a vehicle or a property. The rest of the sum is divided into monthly installments over a period of time.

Revolving credit is the kind that credit cards generally come with. Here you can spend up to a certain credit limit on your card (it will vary from card to card). Once you clear the outstanding amount, you will get fresh credit. In other words, there is always a credit line at your disposal, provided you clear your debts within the period allotted. Along with the interest rate, credit cards also have maintenance and other fees which must be paid. Therefore, before you apply for a credit card, you must understand all the different fees applicable to it, such as:

1. *Annual Fees:* These are charged yearly, like a membership fee for having the card.
2. *Transaction Fees:* The card may charge you for all or certain transactions you make.
3. Balance Transfer Fees: This fee is charged when you transfer balances from one card to another.
4. *Late Payment Fees:* If you fall behind your outstanding payments on your credit card, you will pay this fee as a penalty in addition to the amount outstanding.
5. *Over-Credit-Limit Fees:* If you spend more than the credit limit set on your card, a penalty will be charged to your account.
6. *Return Item Fees:* A penalty is charged whenever a payment is returned for insufficient funds in your account.

Hard and Soft Inquiries

Every time you apply for a loan, your potential creditor will access both your credit score and report. These are called hard inquiries, and too many of these can negatively affect your credit history because it shows that you are trying to open several new lines of credit. Based on this, some lenders may refuse you a loan.

Sometimes, without you actively applying for a loan, a creditor may try to gain information on you through your credit report and score. This will not affect your credit history. For instance, when you access your own credit report, or a landlord does, it will not affect your credit history. These are called soft inquiries.

Why Should You Maintain a Good Credit History?

Good credit will help you in many ways:

- It will help you get future loan approvals faster.
- You can get better terms on loans, like interest rates and charges.
- Potential employers will review your credit history and score. You are more likely to land a good job with a better score.
- Landlords will accept you as a tenant faster if you have a good credit report and score.
- Insurance companies will also review your credit history before accepting your car or home insurance application. They will judge your ability to make the monthly premiums towards the insurance based on your credit report.

A bad credit history with late repayments and bankruptcies will remain on your record for several years, making it extremely difficult to do any of the above. Foreclosures of loans and collections in your name will also show up as bad credit history.

Let us now look at something which will interest many of you: student loans.

A Word on Student Loans

Any student loan you take will inevitably become a part of your credit report. Generally, when you are studying, your loan will show as either "pays as agreed" or "current" on your report. During the grace period, the status will also remain the same. During this time, the payment amount will show $0, as the repayment has not yet begun. Once you start repaying your loan, the status will stay the same. However, the payment amount as per your repayment plan will now be displayed.

If you miss a payment, this will be reflected in your credit report. If you miss or delay too many repayment deadlines, your loan will go into default. The status on your report then changes to "claim has been filed with the government," which means the outstanding amount was settled by a government claim, resulting in a balance of $0. This status can negatively impact your credit history, credit report, and FICO score. As long as this shows on your credit report, you will find it very difficult to open any other line of credit.

How Do You Maintain a Good Credit History and Score?

These are a few ways in which you can maintain a healthy credit history and score:

1. **Credit card limits should be used, but well within limits**. Your credit card history will say a lot about your credit history. It is wise to use about 30% of your credit limit monthly and then settle the bills on time. It also makes sense to keep at least one credit card so that you have a credit history to show.

2. **Increase your credit limit whenever your income and spending go up.** This will ensure that you can manage all your main or recurring expenses on your card and still be within 30% of your credit limit.

3. **Becoming an authorized user of your parents' or a trusted adult's credit card** will improve your credit score. You don't have to use their card or account for this. You must ensure that this friend or relative has a good credit history of making payments on time. This is for people who haven't had much credit history and would like to 'piggy bank' on the good credit history of another.

4. **Settle all your bills and repayments on time**. Delaying or not paying will bring down your score and reflect poorly on your credit history. As you might have observed, your repayment history impacts your credit score the most. You can maintain a physical or digital register of all your payments and even set alarms to remind you to make regular payments on time without missing deadlines. Automation of bank payments will also help to a great extent in this regard.

5. **Don't unnecessarily apply for several loans.** Too many hard inquiries will reflect negatively on your credit history and report.

6. **Review your credit report and dispute mistakes that could reduce your credit score**. You can download your credit report from AnnualCreditReport.com for free once every year. Many people disregard this step, only to find out later that wrong credit information is attributed to them, like payments made on time marked late, or somebody else's bad credit history wrongly ascribed to them, etc. You can also review factors in your favor and elements that are negatively impacting your report.

7. **Monitor your credit score frequently.** Most banks will provide you with this service. The purpose of this is to ensure there are no mistakes in the calculation of your score. You can also check the elements that are bringing down your score and look at options to tackle those. You can also do this through Credit Karma or WalletHub.

8. **Remove delinquencies from your credit report.** If you have a delinquent or collections account, try to have it removed from your credit report once you have paid and closed it as early as possible. For this, you will need to devise a specific action plan for closing this account. Care must be taken so that this does not repeat itself. The more time that passes between the closing of such an account, your credit score will increase.

9. **Consolidate your debts.** If you happen to have several outstanding debts, it is a good idea to try and consolidate them, if possible, at a lower rate of interest. Instead of breaking your head over many small payments, you now have to deal with just a single payment every month. This will make clearing the debt relatively easier for you.

10. **Using a secured credit card is a good way to build your credit score**, as the credit limit is the same as the amount deposited in the account that it is linked to. This shows that you always have an essential balance to clear your credit card dues at any given time. This is a great option for people with no credits or international students who need to build a credit score in the U.S.

11. **Show your rent and utility payments recorded on your credit history.** You can do this using rent reporting services that Equifax, Experian, and Transunion can provide you. A history of paying rent and utility bills on time will help those who otherwise don't have a credit history.

12. **Maintaining several types of credits,** or adding to your credit mix, improves your overall credit score and shows positively on your credit report. Therefore, in addition to the revolving credit on your credit cards, having a history of paying or having paid an installment loan will favor your credit score.

Key Takeaway

Healthy credit history is tied to your financial integrity and how trustworthy a payer you are considered to be. Maintaining a healthy credit score and history will make it easy for you to apply for and get approvals on new loans. This will help you acquire assets like dividend stocks and rental property. These assets, in turn, will allow you to generate passive income. The earlier you start making passive income, the earlier you can retire. The next chapter will give you tips on planning for retirement.

5

RETIREMENT

TIME IS YOUR BEST FRIEND IF YOU START EARLY

How you invest during retirement is as critical as how you invest in preparing for retirement. Things are never as simple and automatic as they once may have been — you worked hard, saved, and then sat back and collected your benefits. You can't rely on someone else coming up with the cash you'll need once you stop working.

DANIEL R. SOLIN

Retirement is often made out to be the sweet fruit of one's labor. All of us are supposed to be aiming for a happy retirement. And when one says "happy," they generally mean "comfortable financially." Retirement need not necessarily mean that one stops working entirely either. The purpose of a fulfilling life is to stay happy. And as far as my experience goes, happy people are those who are happily engaged in what they are doing. There are people who love their jobs so much that retirement is not necessarily a "happily ever after." Thus, if your work keeps you happy, it makes sense for you to prolong your working years and may be consider working part time to make some income during retirement. This way, when you really do have to retire, you can depend on your earnings to an extent.

A few important questions you must ask yourself when it comes to retirement planning. When do you want to retire? What does retirement look like for you? What would you like to do when you retire? Would you still like to pick up some part time work now and then so as not to deplete all your savings and keep you engage with the community? Would you like to start a business or venture of your own that would cushion your retired life but also ensure there is still an active income? Or would you like to not work at all? Remember, these are decisions that are best made for yourself. When it comes to personal finances and life goals, you are the best judge of what is right for you.

Whatever your decision, there is one thing to keep in mind. After retirement, your spending will have to be adjusted against your new earnings. Otherwise, you could put yourself in a difficult financial situation. If you have a retirement benefits plan, like a pension paid out to you, it may not be as high as your last drawn salary. Unlike your salary, there won't be periodic increases, increments, and bonuses. You will have to factor in all these things if you plan to retire or retire early.

At this point, some of you might be thinking. *Hold up! I'm only in my 20s. Why should I have to think about something that's over four decades away?* The truth is happy retirement doesn't just happen. You must plan for it. The key to financial success during retirement is to start investing early. Here's why. If person A starts investing at age 20 and contributes $200 a month until the age of 65, their investment would be worth about $707,532, assuming the stock market return of 7% a year. Under the same market condition, if this person starts investing $200 a month from the age of 25 to 65, their investment would be worth about $494,308. If they start investing at the age of 30, the same investment would only be worth about $342,282. Do you see why investing early is important and how one can easily make a $150,000 mistake by waiting to invest? Given this example, one can conclude that when you start investing matters as much, if not more, than how much you invest.

This chapter looks at a few investing strategies and options you can consider when planning for your retirement and maybe even an early retirement if that's your incentive for a life goal.

The Benefits of 401(k)

It is always great to start your 401(k), i.e., your retirement fund, as early as possible. In most cases, the contribution for this fund is taken from your paychecks and invested into the stock market and bonds. Additionally, many employers match your contribution wholly or partially up to a certain percentage of your salary. Often your 401(k) account and other benefits will be discussed during your onboarding process. You can also inquire with your company's Human Resources regarding setting up this account. When you look at the benefits your company offers, always check for a 401(k) and 401(k) match. The earlier you start funding your 401(k) account, the better, as your investment will experience noticeable growth by the time you reach retirement age.

1. Every contribution you make to a 401(k) account is exempt from tax until you start making withdrawals from it.
2. You will also receive additional free money from employers' match.
3. Contributions are usually automated, so the employee doesn't need to spend additional time and energy making monthly contributions.
4. When checking out options to invest your 401(k) funds, financial experts suggest dividing it into a 4:1 ratio between stocks, which give high returns but are volatile, and bonds which are stable but have lower rates of return.
5. You can start making contributions into your 401(k) account even if you are in the process of paying off debts like student loans. The earlier you contribute to it, the more your retirement fund will grow.
6. You can contribute up to $20,500 in 2022. If you are 50 or older, the limit is $27,000.
7. You can withdraw contributions and earnings without penalty once you reach the age of 59 1/2, though penalty-free withdrawal doesn't mean tax-free. This penalty fee can be waived if you have an unreimbursed deductible medical expense that is greater than 10% of your adjusted gross income or if you become permanently disabled.

Another employment-based retirement account that is closely related to traditional 401(k) is a Roth 401(k). The difference is that the Roth 401(k) contribution comes out of your after-tax paycheck. Because the contribution is made from after-tax money, there is no impact on the current adjusted gross income. However, unlike the traditional 401(k), Roth 401(k)'s tax benefit comes in the later years. Roth 401(k) contributions grow tax-free, and the distribution you withdraw when you reach the minimum age of 59 1/2 is also tax-free.

401(k) Allocation Made Simple

The most crucial choice you must make as you amass retirement funds is how the assets will be invested. How your assets are divided among different asset classes, such as stocks, bonds, and even cash, is called asset allocation. Asset allocation helps lower the risk of losing your investment and increase your returns. Stocks, also known as equities, are generally considered the riskiest investment, though they offer higher potential returns. A stock is an investment that represents the ownership of a fraction of a company. On the other hand, bonds and other fixed-income investments, like certificates of deposits and money market funds, are considered less risky and more conservative with lower returns.

Different asset class performs differently over time. The type of investment portfolio you choose will determine the pace at which your account grows and, subsequently, the money you will be able to withdraw when you retire. Understanding the different investment options, which ones are ideal for you, and how to manage the account moving forward are just a few methods you'll need to employ to maximize your long-term return and minimize the risk while achieving your financial goal.

Typically, your 401(k) plan will offer a selection of investments that is curated by your plan provider and your employer. The risks associated with these investments range from conservative to aggressive. The most common type of fund offered in a 401(k) plan is mutual funds. A mutual fund is an investment vehicle that gathers assets from numerous investors and puts them all into one large pot. The money is then invested in a variety of securities, such as stocks, bonds, commodities, and even real estate, by a qualified fund manager. As an investor, we buy shares in a mutual fund, which represents an ownership interest in the portion of the assets owned by the fund.

There are many different mutual funds to consider. Bond funds, stock funds, balanced funds, and index funds are a few of the popular fund types. Bond funds hold fixed-income securities assets. These bonds provide regular interest to their holders. This interest is distributed to mutual fund holders by the mutual funds. The stock funds are shares of various companies. They are often divided into categories, such as U.S. large-cap, U.S. mid-cap, U.S. small-cap, emerging markets, and international markets. Balanced funds include a mix of bonds and stocks. An index fund is an investment that tracks a market index, such as the S&P 500 or the Nasdaq 100. It is typically made up of stocks and bonds. When you buy an index fund, your money is invested in all the companies that comprise that index, giving you a more diverse portfolio than you would have if you were to purchase individual stocks.

When allocating your asset, you must consider your age, risk tolerance, and your retirement goal. Investors who are in their 20s and have decades to invest before retiring should take a higher risk early on and gradually reduce it as retirement draws near. As a general rule, you may determine the percentage of your portfolio that should be invested in stocks by deducting your age from 110 or 100. Your portfolio will be more aggressive if 110 is used and more conservative if 100 is used. The rest of your portfolio should be invested in bonds. This general rule of thumb is not perfect. Your age and your investment timeline are not the only two factors to consider in your asset allocation. You must know your own risk tolerance.

Ask yourself, "Will you panic sell when the stock market drop by 30%? Or are you the type of investor who can stay calm and ride out the market cycles?" Taking into consideration all these factors will help determine what strategy is best for you.   Below are the three comment models of asset allocations:

Growth portfolio: 70% to 100% in stocks.

Assuming the retirement age of 65, this model is recommended for people younger than 50 who seek higher returns and can tolerate more risk. If you have a higher risk tolerance, you may allocate 100% of your asset to stocks until you reach 40. Between the age of 40 to 50, you can gradually decrease your stock allocation to 80% and increase bonds or other fixed-income assets to 20%. From age 51 to 55, decrease your equities to 70% and increase your fixed-income assets to 30%.

Balanced portfolio: 40% to 60% in stocks.

Assuming the retirement age of 65, this model is recommended when you reach the age of 56 to 60. As one approaches retirement, the balanced portfolio may slowly transition toward an income portfolio. However, if you have lower risk tolerance and the thought of a market downturn keeps you up at night, this type of portfolio might be what you are looking for. This portfolio might not give you a high return like a growth portfolio, but you will sleep better at night knowing your portfolio carries less risk.

Income portfolio: 70% to 100% in bonds.

Assuming the retirement age of 65, this model is recommended for retirees who can't afford the wild swings in the stock market. Though this model is not recommended for younger investors who have decades before retirement; however, if an investor is highly risk-averse, this could be a type of portfolio that they are comfortable with.

Diversifying your portfolio across stocks, bonds, and cash is important in asset allocation because it helps reduce the volatility of your portfolio over time. However, diversification cannot guarantee a profit or protect against loss during a market downturn. In addition to diversifying asset classes, you should also diversify within each asset class. For example, you may include a mixture of different stock funds in your portfolio, such as 40% large-cap, 20% mid-cap, 20% small-cap, and 20% international.

When selecting your investment, it's also crucial to compare investment costs. There are fees involved with maintaining your 401(k) plan account and your investments. Some of these costs are fixed, such as platform costs, recordkeeping costs, etc. Other fees are variable based on the type of investment options you choose. To figure out the costs of your investment, you can look at the expense ratio of the funds. The higher the percentage, the higher the cost. When choosing your fund, you want to choose the fund with lower fees and a return that is on par with the market standard, which is roughly 10% a year.

Below is an example picture of a 401(k) investment election. When you select the fund name, this will bring up information about the particular fund, including its fee, performance, rating, etc. This disclosure document is called a prospectus. There is no limit to how many investments you can elect as long as all the investment percentages add up to 100%. If the thought of picking all these funds feels nerve-racking, overwhelming, and time-consuming, you can always start with a target date fund. Target date fund is a blended fund investment. Thus, it gives you a diversified portfolio. By selecting this one fund, your portfolio will contain U.S. stocks, international stocks, and bonds. The best part about this fund is that as you get closer to retirement age, the fund will automatically re-allocate your investment to less risky assets. Hence, this fund is ideal for passive investors. Target date funds come in various names depending on your 401(k) plan, but they always contain retirement year in their name (ex: CG 2040 TD TD2 or FIOFX 2045). If you are 25 years old and want to retire at 65, you will look at the fund that is 40 years away. For example, it's the year 2022, and you have 40 years until retirement. You will add 2022 with 40, resulting in 2062. There isn't a 2062 target date fund, so you will select 2060 or 2065. It is advised to choose the fund with a later retirement year—in this case, it would be 2065. This is because the target date fund can become too conservative once you get close to retirement age. Due to this reason, it is essential to review your investment at least once a year to make sure that your portfolio still aligns with your financial goal.

Choose Your Investment Elections for: Source Group 1

(Total must equal 100%) **Total: 0%**

Asset Class	Subclass	Fund Name	Current %	Desired %
Blended Fund Investments	--	CG 2020 TD TD2		%
Blended Fund Investments	--	CG 2025 TD TD2		%
Blended Fund Investments	--	CG 2030 TD TD2		%
Blended Fund Investments	--	CG 2035 TD TD2		%
Blended Fund Investments	--	CG 2040 TD TD2		%
Blended Fund Investments	--	CG 2045 TD TD2		%
Blended Fund Investments	--	CG 2050 TD TD2		%
Blended Fund Investments	--	CG 2055 TD TD2		%
Blended Fund Investments	--	CG 2060 TD TD2		%
Blended Fund Investments	--	CG 2065 TD TD2		%
Bond Investments	Stable Value	PRU GUARANTEED INC		%
Bond Investments	Income	FID US BOND IDX		%
Bond Investments	Income	METWEST TOT RTN BD P		%
Bond Investments	Income	PIM REAL RETURN INST		%
Bond Investments	Income	PIMCO INCOME INST		%
Bond Investments	Income	VG TL INTL BD IDX AD		%
Stock Investments	Large Cap	FID 500 INDEX		%
Stock Investments	Large Cap	NB LG CAP VALUE R6		%
Stock Investments	Large Cap	PIONEER FNDML GRTH K		%
Stock Investments	Mid-Cap	FID MID CAP IDX		%
Stock Investments	Mid-Cap	J H ENTERPRISE N		%
Stock Investments	Mid-Cap	JPM MID CAP VALUE R6		%
Stock Investments	Small Cap	DLWR SM CAP CORE R6		%
Stock Investments	Small Cap	FID SM CAP IDX		%
Stock Investments	International	FID GLB EX US IDX		%
Stock Investments	International	INVS DEVELOP MKT R6		%
Stock Investments	International	JHANCOCK INTL GRTH I		%
Stock Investments	International	MFS INTL INTR VAL R6		%
Stock Investments	International	WCM INTL SM CP GR IS		%
Stock Investments	Specialty	AB GLB RE II I		%
Stock Investments	Specialty	PIM COM REAL RET I		%

(Total must equal 100%) **Total: 0%**

Now we have a basic idea of both traditional 401(k) and Roth 401(k) accounts, let us look in detail at Roth IRAs and their benefits.

Roth IRA

Let's start at the very beginning with what the individual retirement account (IRA) is. An IRA is basically a taxable saving in the United States that you can start at any time as long as you have a steady income stream. Once you hit retirement, you can withdraw funds from this account. Similar to 401(k) accounts, IRAs come in two forms: a Roth IRA and a traditional IRA. The main difference between a Roth IRA and a traditional IRA is that the gains and withdrawals from the former are free from the levy of taxes because you already paid taxes on it at the time of contribution. This is especially beneficial for people who think their marginal taxes may increase after retirement.

Many people think that starting a retirement account is only important starting when they get their first paycheck. However, a Roth IRA can be opened much earlier – even for kids and teenagers! Opening such an account early is easy and has many benefits:

1. You can open a Roth IRA at any time, provided you have an active or earned income that particular year. An active or earned income is a salary, bonus, commission, or any earnings you have received for work undertaken or a service provided. The opposite of an active income is a passive income, i.e., income earned from your savings or property, etc.

2. Traditional IRA contributions may be tax-deductible. Traditional IRA contributions are fully tax-deductible if you and your spouse are not covered by an employer retirement plan. A partial deduction may apply if you or your spouse are covered by an employer retirement plan, and you make less than a certain income threshold. Unlike traditional IRAs, the Roth IRA is not tax-deductible as you contribute to the account with your after-tax money. However, the contribution in Roth IRA grows tax-free and once you start making withdrawals from this account, they are exempt from tax.

3. Adults can contribute to a Roth IRA in the name of a child or teenager. Currently, there is no minimum age limit for a Roth account in a child's name. Technically, parents or guardians can even open such an account for newborn babies. However, the child or teen will have to show an income equaling or exceeding the contribution into the account. For very young children, such an income generally comes from modeling or acting.

4. There is a contribution limit to a Roth IRA. As of 2020, people below 50 years of age can deposit a maximum of $6,000 into their Roth IRA per year. Those who are above 50 can deposit up to $7,000 annually.

5. When opening an account in the name of a minor (a person below 18, 19, or 21 years, depending on the state to which they belong), the adult opening it on their behalf will have custodial rights to the funds until the minor comes of age. Otherwise, these accounts will have the same functionality and mode of operation as when they are in the name of an adult. Sometimes the minimum limits on deposits into the account of a minor may be lower than that of an adult.

6. The earnings on such accounts are calculated at interest rates that are compounded. Thus, a person who makes a single deposit of $5,000 at the age of 15 can earn over $269,000 in 50 years.

7. The Roth IRA is a great way for a teenager who makes an income to start saving early. They will receive great benefits by the time they plan their retirement at around 55 or 60 years of age.

8. Similar to 401(k), when you fund your IRA accounts, you will have to invest your funds in different types of assets. The most common IRA investments tend to be mutual funds. Buying a low-cost U.S. stock fund and a low-cost U.S. bond fund will provide you with sufficient diversification to optimize your returns and minimize the risk. Some examples of good low-cost U.S. index funds for IRA accounts are Vanguard S&P 500 ETF, iShares Core S&P 500 ETF, SPDR S&P 500 ETF Trust, and Fidelity ZERO Large Cap Index.

The following is a comparison between the Roth IRA and the regular IRA. Decide which is best for you based on the table below.

Aspect	Roth IRA	Traditional IRA
Early Withdrawals from any retirement account are discouraged and will attract a penalty or a fine.	There is more flexibility for early withdrawals before the term of the account.	Heavy fines as much as 10% of the value of the account are levied in the case of early withdrawals.
Minimum Distribution	The Roth IRA doesn't have as many restrictions on the account holder. In most cases, you can decide how long to let your investment grow in the account.	It requires retirees to make the required minimum distributions by the time they reach 72 years.
Tax Benefit	Since you receive the tax benefit after retirement, you would be more prudent in saving it.	Since tax benefits are received when you are still earning and contributing to the account, you may be tempted to spend those savings on unnecessary things.
Tax Benefits with a 401(k) company-sponsored retirement benefits scheme.	Similar to Roth 401(k), Roth IRA provides you similar options for better tax savings.	Tax benefits on a 401(k) and traditional IRAs are almost the same.

The sections above have hinted at the importance of starting retirement funds early. However, most of the information above has been in the context of the United States. Let us now look at how you can build a retirement fund in Canada, the United Kingdom, and Australia. The following sections will be helpful for those who are seeking to emigrate to any of these countries in the long run. However, you may skip this section if it does not apply to you.

Retirement Schemes Abroad

The Roth IRA in Canada

A Roth IRA can be held by Canadians either in the US or via Canadian brokers who manage US accounts. Now let us look at some rules for holding such accounts in Canada:

1. You can bring your Roth IRA to Canada, and if you make the suitable tax choices, you can have a full tax deferral on the account as well. However, many brokers may not be qualified to work within both Canadian and US investment accounts. Thus, many will simply decline to work with them.

2. Canadians can hold Roth IRAs legally. However, these could be considered foreign financial accounts and may need to be declared on Canadian Foreign Disclosure forms.

3. Under the Canada US Tax Treaty, a Roth IRA is tax-exempt. Though traditional IRA and 401(k) accounts needn't be reported under Canada's foreign income verification rules, it remains unclear whether this is applicable to Roth accounts.

4. There are special Roth IRA elections that one would have to file with the Canada Revenue Agency (CRA) to maintain the tax exemption on Roth IRA Accounts. The following are the details that you would have to file:

- Your name and address
- Your Social Insurance Number and Social Security Number
- Name of the plan holder
- Date the plan was started
- Date of becoming a Canadian resident
- Balance of the Roth IRA in December 2008, or when you became a Canadian resident
- Amount and date of the first Canadian contribution to the Roth IRA

- A statement of election to defer tax on the account under paragraph seven, article XVIII of the Canada-US Income Tax Treaty

5. Once the above election has been made, the account holder should ensure no further contributions are made to the Roth IRA.

Some more facts related to Roth IRA accounts in Canada:

1. The Canadian equivalent of the Roth IRA does exist and is called The Canadian Tax-Free Savings Account (or TFSA). Though similar, the particular tax applications on it could vary.
2. Maintaining your Roth IRA is beneficial even if you decide to move to Canada, as withdrawals from it would continue to be tax-free.
3. It may make sense to move your funds from a traditional IRA or a 401(k) into a Roth IRA for tax benefits. However, before you make such a move, get it reviewed and approved by a financial advisor, mainly because this would now come under the purview of cross-border investment.
4. You can bequeath your Roth IRA account via a will to beneficiaries, who can then let it grow over a lifetime. If you have owned your account for over five years, this transfer will be tax-free.
5. There is no provision at present to convert your Roth IRA into a Canadian government-approved Registered Retirement Savings Plan (RRSP). However, traditional IRAs and 401(k) can be converted to an RRSP.

Next, we shall look at how one can tackle retirement in the UK.

Retirement Plans in the UK

There are several retirement pension options available to people residing in the UK. Let us look at the two main kinds of pension plans that are most commonly availed of, i.e., private vs. state pensions.

Private Pension	Type	What is it?
	Workplace pensions	These are arranged by your employer. Usually both you and your employer make deposits into it. Based on the type of scheme your employer offers, you get a sum every month after you retire.
	Personal and stakeholder pensions	This is a private pension that you contribute to. Employers can also pay into them as part of a workplace pension scheme. Based on how much is paid in and how well the investment does, you get a sum every month after you retire.
State Pension	New State Pension	This is a regular payment you can get from the government when you reach State Pension age. The amount you get will be based on National Insurance contributions and credits. The full new State Pension amount is £185.15 per week.
	Protected payment	Any amount over the full new State Pension of £185.15 that you get from your National Insurance contributions is protected, which means that it will be paid on top of the full new State Pension amount.
	Pension Credit	For people on a low income, this scheme tops up your weekly income to £182.60 for single persons, or £278.70 for couples. If you're a caregiver, are disabled, are responsible for a child, or have certain housing costs, you may get more.

Some other features of UK government work laws related to retirement are:

1. You can work past the state pension age and are protected by law in this choice. At this stage, you don't have to pay national insurance.
2. There is no official retirement age in the UK, and employers cannot make employees redundant solely

on their age criteria. However, in certain circumstances, employers can set the retirement age.

3. Normally applications for jobs need not mention your age. This is to prevent ageism. Employers are also disallowed from setting age limits unless the job role involves specific skills like physical fitness, etc.

4. To get more help, you can check out government-sponsored links: MoneyHelper will assist you in getting advice on your retirement options. PensionWise has personal assisted services for you if your money is in a 'defined contribution' pension plan.

5. If you're paying into a pension scheme, you sometimes may withdraw up to £500 to pay for financial advice on retirement. You can do this one-three times a year without a tax charge. Not all pension schemes provide this, so it's best to discuss your options with your pension provider on this.

Now that we have looked at options in the UK let us also look at similar options available in Australia.

Investing for Retirement in Australia

In Australia, some schemes will help you plan your retirement. These are usually termed 'superannuation', or just 'super', and are used instead of retirement pension benefit funds.

1. How much money you'll need to retire: this will depend on what your costs could look like after you retire and for how long you'd need them. Generally, we tend to retire around 65 years and may live for another 20 years. Your super would need to cover

such expenses as medical bills, travel, and mortgage or rent, apart from others.

2. Your retirement income can come from your super, investments and savings, government benefits, or even your home if you downsize.

3. It is a good idea to consolidate your super into one account. Hence, you pay fewer fees, make additional contributions to grow your super, and change your super investment options for better growth.

4. Your super can be withdrawn as an account-based pension, an annuity, a lump sum amount, or a combination of the three.

At this stage, I would quickly like to draw your attention to the similarities and differences between 401(k) in the USA vs. Australia's superannuation schemes.

Super in Australia vs. the 401(k) in the United States

In the table below, you will find the points of difference between the two retirement schemes in Australia and the USA.

Super in Australia	401(k) in the USA
Superannuation is mandatory in Australia.	401(k) is a voluntary scheme in which an employee can choose to join.
All employees are entitled to superannuation which is calculated currently at 10.5% of an employee's gross salary.	An employee who chooses a 401(k) has a percentage deducted from their paycheck into an investment account. The employer can match some or all of that amount.
Super is paid by your employer on top of the salary you make.	401(k) contributions are deducted from your monthly paycheck.
Super contributions in Australia are taxed at 15%. Withdrawals are also taxed based on whether they are a part of a taxed or untaxed super fund. Those who withdraw from their super will generally pay 15%-45% tax.	401(k) plans are tax-deferred, meaning you don't pay taxes until you withdraw the funds that become a part of your taxable income.
Employees can top up their account after income taxes have been deducted using non-concessional contributions so that withdrawals and earnings are not subject to tax.	After-tax contributions can be made by employees to their retirement plan with a Roth 401(k) plan.
Before-tax contributions are capped at $27,500, while the non-concessional contribution limit is $110,000.	The 401(k)-contribution limit is $20,500USD, and for those over 50 years, there is an additional catch-up available of $6,500USD, totalling $27,000. The overall annual contributions cannot exceed $61,000USD (or $67,500USD including catch-up).
A person can only withdraw super when they retire, reach the preservation age (even if they are still working) or if they undergo specific conditions, such as severe financial hardship, disability, or illness.	You can't withdraw from your 401(k) early without attracting a 10% penalty. You can access or partly withdraw a 401(k) distribution early if you meet certain conditions, like early retirement or losing your job at 55 years or older. Otherwise, you can't access your 401(k) until you turn 59.5 years old.
People need not make withdrawals from their super even after they retire. However, they can't make personal contributions once they are over 75 years of age.	A person must receive distributions from their plans when they retire and reach 72 years of age.
Employees can choose their own super fund and investment option (choices range between high-growth assets like domestic and global shares, to low-risk investments such as fixed interest and cash). Workers can also opt for their employer's choice of super fund, which is the company's default investment option.	Employees are in control of their investments, but they choose from a selection offered by their employer. These usually include mutual and target-date funds, as well as guaranteed investment contracts (GICs) or shares in the company they work for (Gjorgievska, 2022).

So much for the technical aspects of retirement benefits. Let us now look at a simple calculation that might help you to decide when you can retire.

The Math Behind Early Retirement

This section will provide a simple hack to determine your retirement age based on your savings rate as a percentage of your take-home income. Your savings rate should be based on two figures – your income and what you can live on.

Now, this is not some genius equation I came up with. It was first outlined in a blog titled "The Shockingly Simple Math Behind Early Retirement" by Mr. Money Mustache in 2012. And before you dismiss this as some bogus financial guru, you can also read several other blogs and articles by financial enthusiasts who have backed up these figures. The blog "Does Mr. Money Mustache's Shockingly Simple Math Hold Up?" by Matthew in 2021, who is also a personal finance mentor, corroborates the original figures of the earlier blog. The following is an adaptation of the table that would suggest when you can retire.

Savings Rate	Number of Years to Be Worked Until Retirement
10	51
20	37
30	28
40	22
50	17
60	12.5
70	8.5
80	5.5
90	Less than 3
100	0

There are some points that must be assumed while using this table:

1. You must earn 5% investment returns after inflation during your saving years.

2. You'll live off 4% of the retirement fund after retirement, allowing some leeway for your spending during recessions.

3. You will only use the gains on your investments as you cannot afford to deplete your assets themselves.

This table is just one way of deciding whether you are saving what you ought to be, how far away retirement is, and if you can live off the assets you have created.

Key Takeaway

I know there is quite a bit of information covered in this section. I hope one thing you will do is start putting money toward an investment account, like a 401k or an IRA account. Retirement can sound far away, but planning and taking action early is vital in securing your financial future. This is important not just for you but for everyone who is and will be dependent on you. When discussing your future, another critical aspect of managing your risks before retirement is looking into insurance schemes that suit your purpose. But more about that in the next chapter.

6

INSURANCE

THE ONLY THINGS THAT SOUNDS RIDICULOUS UNTIL YOU NEED IT

Nothing is more important than your life and your ability to make a living. So it makes good sense to insure your greatest asset – you!

BT AUSTRALIA

J ames Otis Jr. was an activist for the newly independent America of the late 1770s. You may have heard of him with reference to one of the revolutionary cries that shook up Great Britain in those times: "no taxation without representation." The slogan, attributed to him, would later symbolize justice from the government in exchange for the loyalty of its subjects. In his prime, Mr. Otis was a firebrand orator. In later years, he is alleged to have lost his mind. The world also remembers him for another reason. Family lore has it that he foretold his own death. He called upon God to end his days by striking him with lightning, and that is exactly what happened! On 23 May 1783, when he was 58 years of age, as he was speaking to a group of people by the doorway of a friend's home, he was struck by lightning. What is remarkable is that nobody else was injured. It seemed too amazing to be true.

Unlike Mr. Otis, not everyone has the good or bad fortune to know when and how they will be called back into the oblivion they came from. Thus, in life, it makes sense to follow the maxim "hope for the best and prepare for the worst." Before you dismiss me as some harbinger of ill will, let me remind you that I am in no way promoting morbidity. Far from it – this entire book has been an exercise in living to the fullest and reaping the best from it.

In the previous chapters, we have dealt with budgeting, saving, clearing debts, and improving credit reputation. This section of the book will look at securing the most critical asset in your possession to date – your life. We will also take into account other assets that would be in your best interest to insure. This way, you will always be prepared for losses as you climb new heights professionally and personally. The following section will look at what kinds of insurance you should consider.

The Kinds of Insurance Policies That Must Be Considered

The thing puzzling most newbies to the world of wealth creation tends to be, "What are the things I must secure against damage or loss?" This will be followed by questions like, "Does it make sense for me to spend on something I may not need?" and "Why add to my existing tax and other liabilities?"

The following sections will shed some light on why insurance is not actually the liability or burden it is so often perceived to be.

Life insurance is, as the term suggests, insuring your life against ailments and death. Obviously, since the elixir of life has eluded both science and magic, I do not suggest that insurance will magically help anyone live forever.

However, we all have the power to make the blow of a physical handicap, ailment, or death less severe on our beloved or dependents by opting for a sound life or health insurance plan. Such forms of insurance will cover all major costs related to such eventualities so that, in addition to bereavement, you need not put your family through the burden of wading and sorting through financial knots and the anxiety of making ends meet.

Let us now look at four types of insurance policies that are most commonly sought:

Life Insurance

Life insurance is a payout to your family in the case of your death. Financial experts suggest that the payout from a life insurance policy should ideally be ten times your annual income. However, such a policy could work out to be pretty expensive in terms of the premiums you would have to pay. To work out a comfortable life insurance policy, you must keep in mind the following expenses, especially if your family is completely dependent on your salary:

1. Funeral expenses and death dues
2. Rental or mortgage payments
3. Outstanding loans or credit card dues
4. Childcare or future college fees
5. Taxes
6. The average rate of inflation

Keeping these figures in mind, you can arrive at a sum that would cover the expenses and liabilities incurred after your death. If you know the payout that would be necessary, you can work backward with the help of an insurance agent to arrive at the monthly premiums you would have to pay.

There are two main types of life insurance covers:

1. **Permanent life policy:** You will pay your premiums until the end of your life, and your nominee(s) will receive the payout on your death. This type of policy usually also includes a cash value component.

2. **Term life policy:** You pay a premium for a fixed period, which could be anywhere between 5-40 years. After this period, the policy expires. If you expire before the term period is over, there will be an agreed payout to your nominee(s) as per the agreement made. If you don't die within the term specified in your policy, it expires with no payout.

When choosing between these two types of life insurance covers, it is best to consult a financial expert who will take into account factors such as age, health, and occupation before suggesting a wise course of action for you.

Along with the above common forms of life insurance, there are other forms of life insurance, such as final expense insurance, group life insurance, and endowment policy. Final expense insurance is a form of life insurance that is only meant to pay for end-of-life expenses, such as funeral and burial charges. Group life insurance is generally offered as an employment-based benefit. Premiums are determined by the entire group instead of an individual. Company typically provides basic coverage without charge as an employee perk, and employees have the option to purchase additional coverage if they require extra protection. Endowment plans are similar to term plans, except that there is a guaranteed sum assured after the term. If, during the term, the insured person expires, the nominee(s) will receive the sum assured, plus a bonus. If the insured outlives the term, they will still get the sum assured as a payout. This plan is beneficial when planning things in advance, like your children's education, etc.

In some instances, certain life insurance, like indexed universal life insurance (IUL) and variable life insurance (VUL), can also offer the benefits of both insurance and investment. In other countries outside the U.S., this type of insurance may also be called Unit Linked Insurance Plan (ULIP). With this insurance, a portion of the premium will be tied to investment accounts, like, stocks, bonds, or both, and will provide you with regular returns. However, these plans might also involve market risks, as all investments in stocks or bonds are liable. With partial withdrawals and other features, these policies offer more flexibility and tax benefits than traditional insurance policies; however, due to the duality of them being both investment and insurance, they have high management fees for the first five to ten years of the policy. They are considered long-term investments; hence, they are NOT generally recommended for everyone.

Health Insurance

According to official records from the Centers for Disease Control, 9.2% of Americans have no health coverage at all. Most Americans have an employer or the government subsidizing or sponsoring their health care through insurance. Despite this, research showed that 60% of Americans who filed for bankruptcy cited medical costs as one of the primary causes of their financial decline (Konish, 2019). According to the same study, around 530,000 families have declared bankruptcy owing to medical costs. Having health coverage will ensure that you can have timely health checkups without incurring huge bills. In case of an accident or illness, again, a good health insurance coverage will keep you and your loved ones financially secure.

There are five factors you should consider when choosing health insurance:

1. **Type of plan and provider network.** Some plans only cover in-network providers and may partially cover out-of-network providers. Make sure to check if your health care providers, hospitals, and pharmacies you prefer are within the plan's network.

2. **Premiums.** What will your monthly insurance cost be? Premium is how much you will pay monthly for the coverage. Most children and young adults in the U.S. are covered by their parent's job-based insurance. This coverage usually ends when one turns 26. Additionally, most colleges in the U.S. also require their students to have health insurance. If the plan you have does not satisfy your university's eligibility requirements, you may have to opt for the insurance plan that the school provides. Once you start working with a company that provides health benefits, you can obtain health insurance through your employer. Your premium would be deducted biweekly from your paycheck.

3. **Deductibles.** How much will you pay out of your pocket before the insurance starts to cover your

medical expenses? If you have $1,500 deductibles, your health plan won't pay for your medical expenses until you have paid $1,500 out of pocket. These expenses may include office visits, procedure fees, lab tests, and prescriptions. Most plans are required by law to cover eligible preventative services, such as vaccines, screening tests, and annual physical checkups, at no cost to you. If your plan covers preventative care, it would be wise to take advantage of the service.

4. **Coinsurance or Co-pay.** In addition to premiums and deductibles, you should also consider the additional charge that you may be responsible for to access care. Coinsurance is a percentage of medical charges you must pay, typically after you reach the deductible. For example, if you have 30% coinsurance. Your plan will pay 70% of the cost, and you will pay 30%. Co-pay is a flat fee you will pay every time you have a doctor visit or fill a prescription. Your co-pay does not count toward your deductible. You are responsible for coinsurance and co-pay even after you reach your deductible. This cost-sharing stops when your combined medical expenses reach your out-of-pocket maximum, though you'll still have to continue paying the premiums.

5. **Medical Coverage.** What is covered by the insurance plan? When choosing a policy, you have to make sure that most, if not all, of your medical expense needs are met. Cosmetic surgeries, infertility or pregnancy-related complication, hearing, vision, and dental may not be covered by your health insurance. Furthermore, your regular prescription also may not be covered. Your insurance may only cover its

generic alternative, or they may offer partial coverage with a co-pay or coinsurance.

Health insurance can be expensive. For employees, the best option is generally to stick to the employer-sponsored health care policy. If you fall under a low-income category, it is still possible to have insurance coverage. You may be eligible for government plans such as Medicare, Medicaid, and the Children's Health Insurance Program (CHIP).

Long-Term Disability Coverage

Most of us are convinced that we will never require benefits from such a policy because what are the odds of getting handicapped? But this is not something that should be so easily overlooked. Social Security statistics reveal that in the private sector, 65% of the workforce has no long-term disability insurance, and about one in four people who are 20-year-olds today will become disabled before they turn 67. Thus, they will be unable to continue working owing to this disability.

This coverage will help you earn even if you are in the hospital and/or your disability prevents you from working. Without it, you may find yourself having to dip into your savings to cover daily living expenses for yourself and your family. This is why some employees opt for both short- and long-term disability coverage, among other employee benefits. This policy will yield as much as 40-70% of one's income, depending upon the scheme one opts for. The premiums or costs of disability coverage will be based on one's age, occupation, health, and lifestyle. It usually does not exceed 1-3% of your annual salary.

As beneficial as such a policy can be, always read the fine print, as there are policies that don't pay out for three months or more after making the request. There are also policies that don't offer more than three years of coverage and have significant exclusions in the policy terms.

Auto Insurance

If you don't have vehicle insurance, you will be responsible for the financial losses incurred after an accident. There are several benefits to having auto insurance. It helps secure your car against theft, damage, and even natural disasters. In case of an accident, it will secure your interest, such as expenses against damage and litigation charges, if any. Almost all states in the U.S., except New Hampshire, mandate vehicle insurance.

As with any other insurance policy, you can check quotes from different agencies and verify if you are eligible for policies that will cost you less. Make sure to shop around.

Why Insure While Still Young?

Most people equate insurance with old age and death; therefore, many people are reluctant to take on an insurance policy until much later in life. However, when you insure yourself and your assets early, not only will the cost be less, but you will also get the advantage of a longer-running coverage policy and the safety net it offers. Let us now look at specific reasons why you ought to ensure your assets and your life at the earliest time possible:

1. As a young adult, you have more "adulting" responsibilities than when you were in your teens. It's also very likely that you may not have a substantial emergency fund to fall back on yet. Some of you might have just started working. Others might be supporting their parents and siblings who are perhaps

just starting school. You might also start your own family. If something were to happen to you, you might not have the contingency savings to cover the expenses and take care of the people who depend on you. If you are insured, some, if not all, of your financial burden will be alleviated.

2. The earlier you take on health or life insurance, the lower the premiums will be. Every time you apply for personal insurance, you need to complete a health checkup and lifestyle-related questionnaire. These assess your age and state of health. The healthier and fitter you are, the less chance you have of you falling sick or dying, and the premium tends to be low. Even if you have no ailments, the premium increases with your age.

3. If you select a scheme like the ULIP and IUL, the benefits of compounding will help you earn a higher return on investment over a longer timeframe. Suppose you invest in insurance in your 20s versus your 40s – if the policy matures when you are 60 years of age, the interest you earn will compound over a period of 35 years or more in the first case, compared to only around 15 years in the second case.

4. You can insure yourself against the potential loss of income due to factors outside your control. Job loss insurance and supplemental unemployment insurance will provide you with a steady income if you were let go without fault by your employer. In this way, your basic expenses can be taken care of even as you search for your next job.

How Do I Choose the Best Plan for Me?

Before you narrow down a policy, ask yourself the following questions. They will help you determine your priorities and the most important financial obligations to cover in case something happens to you.

1. What's your current financial situation? What are your monthly expenses, and how much savings do you have?
2. What are my long-term goals? Do I plan to take out a student loan or to study further? Do I plan to marry and settle down? The insurance policy should cover your main targets, depending on your answers to these questions.
3. How many dependents do I have: aging parents, children, a spouse? These questions will enable you to decide on a suitable payout to cover all the necessary living expenses.
4. Do I have any current or upcoming liabilities? This is something your dependents may not be able to cover in your absence, and it might require a policy.
5. What health or other problems can I account for in my policy? With small additional payments, some insurance policies offer you protection against illness, handicaps, and income loss. You could consider some of them.

Let us now consider the important question of when you may need assistance with financial planning.

Is a Financial Advisor Necessary? How Do I Find the Right
Person?

The next most important question to ask yourself is whether
you need a financial advisor or planner. If you are financially
capable, I suggest that you find such a person who can take on
some of the burdens of deciding the right policy and financial
investments for you. Such a person will be able to calculate
your exact needs and requirements and can help you choose
affordable options that will provide you with the best coverage
and returns. Hiring an advisor is a personal choice and
different people will find different values in having an advisor.
For many young adults, a financial advisor is not necessary,
because our financial situation is not too complicated.
However, down the road when you start to earn more, acquire
more assets, or receive a large inheritance, seeking out professional help might be worth the time and money.

Here are some preliminary steps to take to ensure you find a
financial advisor who is suited to your requirements:

1. **Decide whether having an advisor is really
    necessary.** If your asset base is small and you have
    the time and energy to do your own research and
    create your own financial plans, as well as decide on
    how to best ensure your assets against loss, you can
    save on hiring a financial advisor. Once you become a
    high-income earner with sizable assets and managing
    these assets starts to feel like a part-time job, you may
    consider looking for a financial advisor to guide you.
    By logical reasoning, your assets will continue to grow,
    and getting help from an experienced professional can

free up your time and energy to create more wealth. The National Association of Personal Financial Advisors can help you find an advisor who will suit you. Visit www.napfa.org.

2. **Consider what you need help with.** Not all financial planners can provide specialized knowledge on all financial needs. What areas do you need assistance in? Perhaps you need help managing your assets, choosing investments, or taking out an insurance policy. Some advisors will help you with financial analysis, estate planning, retirement planning, etc. Based on your needs, you can narrow down your search.

3. **There are several types of advisors to pick from.** Therefore, it's important to know what help you need and what kind of advisor would be best equipped to assist you. There are traditional financial advisors, and those who consult online, and even robo-advisors. The cost of consulting can vary greatly, depending on the services you seek. The following chart can be used for general reference if you are in doubt about the kind of advisors you need:

Traditional Advisors	Online/Hybrid Advisors	Robo-advisors
People with whom you can build a relationship.	Firms or individuals who provide you flexible interaction either face to face or online.	Not much human interaction. This service uses computer algorithms to build and manage clients' portfolios.
They can provide you with personalized solutions to more complex financial problems.	They can provide you with solutions; however, with the mix of online and offline interaction, you might not be working with just one advisor. This could limit you to a narrower scope of financial advice than the holistic financial planning that is available when you are working with just one advisor.	Solutions for easy cases where human intervention is not necessary. It may not suit you if you have particular or specific questions or need more comprehensive financial planning.
This might sound ageist; however, you may want to consider the age of the advisor. If you are looking for someone to work on a long-term basis, you may not want someone who will be retiring soon. However, the upside is that the longer they are in the industry, the more experience they have, and even if they end up retiring, they may be able to refer you to another trusted advisor.	Some hybrid financial services will match you with one dedicated advisor. However, it's more likely that you will be working with multiple. Hence, there is no danger of losing them.	You will always have access to them as long as you have access to the internet.
Generally expensive because you are paying for their expertise.	Not as expensive as an individualized financial advisory system, but more expensive than automated options.	The most cost friendly type of financial advice one can receive.

4. **In addition to considering virtual or in-person advising, you also must consider if you want a captive or independent advisor.** Captive advisors are those who work for a firm. Because they work for an organization, many of the administrative tasks are taken care of by the

firm. Hence, they have more time to focus on relationship building with clients. The downside is that captive advisors are limited to only selling the products and services of the company they work for, and these products may not wholly serve your purpose. Independent advisors, on the hand, have more diverse options for the products and services they can provide. Thus, they may be able to combine various products that are best tailored to your need. However, because they are independent advisors, their time may also be split for administrative tasks, such as building their client lists and advertising. They also may not have a substantial budget for market research and product innovation. Because they are strictly commission-based, there might be an incentive for them to push for products that are more costly to their clients. Thus, you have to do your research and find reviews of the advisors you want to work with. A bad financial advisor can have a conflict of interest and squander your hard-earned money in hidden fees and commissions. With the legalese and hidden provisions buried in financial paperwork, it can be difficult to discern who has your best financial interest. Here are some tips to help you out:

- Learn to differentiate between fiduciary and non-fiduciary financial advisors. Fiduciary advisors are also called "fee-only" advisors, and they won't claim a commission against your earnings. They will work on your behalf with a "client always comes first" attitude. Because they are paid only by you and clients like you, they have no conflict of interest that comes with commission-based advisors. They will generally provide you with the best possible financial advice.
- Non-fiduciary or suitability advisors are legally bound to give you sound financial advice but make no claims to give you the best possible financial advice. They

may recommend you a product for which they receive a commission or other type of compensation for the sale, hence lining their pockets in the process.

5. **Assessing what you can spend on financial advice will help you to decide whom to approach.** Generally, financial advisors are paid via a fee, commission, or a combination of both. Be very clear about these charges before you hire an advisor.

6. **Verify your advisor's credentials, and get referrals via the internet or, better yet, through trusted friends.** This will help prevent you from making a financial decision that's not in your best interest. You can check the credentials of your advisor or the consulting firm via free online sites like BrokerCheck.finra.org or AdviserInfo.sec.gov. You can also check up on Google or enlist the help of friends who can direct you toward reliable and trusted experts in the field.

7. **Take your time to select your advisor by meeting and interviewing many candidates.** You don't need to make a decision immediately; you can wait to find a candidate with whom you can work in the long run. You should check for integrity, clarity in communication, and ease of access before finalizing your financial advisor. Ensure that the expert you choose has well-documented practices in place before you hire them. One way of doing this would be to speak to the clients of an advisor to see how satisfied they are with the services being provided if possible.

Hopefully, the above makes it clearer for you to decide whether you need financial planning and what kind of advisor you might consider helping you manage, grow, or save your asset base.

Key Takeaway

This chapter has provided you with the knowledge essential for picking the right insurance policies and financial management team who will help you invest, grow, and save your assets, thus helping you attain your specific financial goals and targets. Like a retirement plan, insurance covers yield the best possible results when chosen earlier rather than later. However, any financial securement plan you enter also requires you to plan your income so you can meet their monthly or yearly costs and premiums. The following chapter will deal with how to reinforce your income, and thereby your earning potential, via a passive income.

7

INVEST

BECAUSE A PENNY SAVED IS NOT A PENNY EARNED

An investment in knowledge pays the best interest.

BENJAMIN FRANKLIN

L et me hark back to the Parable of the Talents that I mentioned in the introduction of this book. In the Bible, "talents" is a thinly veiled reference to one's natural abilities in various things like music, art, writing, or any other pursuit. It must be assumed from Jesus' story that refusing to grow one's talents or to work towards fulfilling one's potential is nothing short of a crime for which one can incur God's wrath. Now, I am not preaching fire and brimstone as the consequences of refusing to work toward asset growth. However, I believe that anyone who aims at any kind of growth should also be committed to financial growth. Let's face it, money may not be everything in life, but it can give you freedom and choices. Imagine waking up every day and being able to do whatever you want, whenever you want, with whomever you want. Money brings comfort if not precisely happiness. You can work towards other fulfillment in life more easily when money isn't a problem, and you are not grinding every day merely to afford necessities. It makes sense then to work towards your financial freedom, doesn't it?

The right investment toward a happy financial future can only proceed through investing in the proper knowledge, and that is, in part, my aim for this chapter. Though I do not own a real estate property myself yet, from my research, it is one of the best long-term investments. Over the last two centuries, about 90% of millionaires around the world have amassed their wealth through real estate. Though real estate is not as liquid as stocks and may require more money and time, it offers other benefits that you won't find in other types of investments. These benefits include but are not limited to monthly cash flow, tax advantages, and protection against inflation.

One of the major areas that this chapter will cover is how early investment in real estate can change the whole ball game for an investor in terms of financial growth. We will also cover different strategies for wealth creation in real estate.

Real Estate is the Real Deal

Many people neglect real estate because, generally, it is not one of the easy hacks that support the "get-rich-quick" dream of one's youth and could have a high financial barrier to entry. It is true that compared to other modes of investment, real estate investments are kinder to those who patiently wait than those who are in a hurry to get quick results.

The real estate market tends to dip and pick up again over time, and quick dips and slight falls will not affect you if you hold on to the asset for a number of years. Over time, real estate, like the stock market and other investment options, tends to make remarkable profits for the holder. The earlier you start investing, the longer you can hold on to a property and witness its growth.

The biggest pro to real estate is that, unlike stocks, rental values don't dip as much during recession periods, and you can still make a good income by investing in it.

The Earlier, the Better

In the case of investing in real estate, getting started is half the battle won. If you follow sound advice, you can steer clear of big mistakes and have a lifetime of honing your skills so you can make the best profits in the trade.

We will now look at the various ways in which you can make a start:

- **Get the right education.** Learning about real estate and how it works should be one of your priorities if you want to make a profit from it. Start by getting your hands on articles, blogs, books, podcasts, and videos. A search on Google will give you varieties of resources on the subject. If you would like a more specialized approach, you can enroll in an online course or workshop. The key is to choose resources, websites, and other materials that are reliable and vetted by professionals.
- **Make a financial plan.** Real estate requires quite a lot of investment upfront. Thus, it is vital to make an

extra income to boost your savings if you want to buy property or land. If this is not viable for you at the moment, consider whether you can team up with a trusted partner who can work with you and fund your dreams or consider real estate investing strategies, such as wholesaling and Airbnb rental arbitrage.

- **Build a partnership.** A trusted partner may be able to fund the project, but you must ensure that you bring the brains and energy for the deal. When one person contributes financially, the other will have to see to the nitty gritty of the process. It won't be a bad deal if the two of you have your responsibilities decided upon and sharing the profits is clearly chalked out from the beginning.

- **Gain experience by volunteering or interning with an experienced real estate company or brokerage.** When you bring the right knowledge and zeal to the table, a financial partner will be easier to find.

Once the above is in place, you can get cracking and start your investment journey in real estate.

Let us now look at specific ways in which you can invest in the real estate market:

1. **House hacking** involves buying a multifamily property for which the mortgage is partly paid by the rent from tenants. For instance, you can buy a property and rent out a room to a tenant, who would pay you monthly. You can also buy a property with more than one floor and use one for living while tenants use the other floors. House hacking offers the following advantages:

- If you want to buy a property solely as an investment, most banks require at least 20% as a down payment. They know that an owner is more likely to default on payments when they don't stay at the property. However, the down payment could be much smaller if you take a loan from Veterans Affairs (VA) or the Federal Housing Administration (FHA) (Albaum, 2021). Of course, this will depend on your credit score, income, etc. You will also have to pay Private Mortgage Insurance until you reach 20% equity in your property holdings.
- The interest rate on private home loans is lower than on commercial properties. Thus, buying private property saves money in terms of the loan amount to be paid.
- You will learn to become self-reliant when repairing things around the place because you live there. Basic repairs, painting, and other things like replacing bulbs or broken tiles can be done by you. This will save the money you would otherwise have to spend on repair services.
- House hacking is less risky than getting into a complete rental agreement because if you rent out your entire property, your rental income will have to cover everything from the mortgage to the property tax and even your own rent. When you stay in the home you have purchased and rent out a portion of it, your mortgage can be covered by the renter, and you are also the landlord, who can set rules on how your property would be managed.

2. **House flipping** involves buying a fixer-upper home, and repairing, modifying, and improving it so you can sell it for a

profit. This will require quite a bit of money to be spent on renovation, insurance, rent, utility bills, and marketing. How can the buyer meet all those expenses until they flip and sell it? The answer is through lenders. Based on your need, you can contact the following types of lenders:

- Private money lenders charge more interest than institutions like banks. However, the process is much simpler and quicker than a traditional home loan, which can take over a month for the loan to be sanctioned. The other benefit of private money lenders is that they might offer you the entire value of the property, so you need not actually spend anything out of your pocket for the purchase.
- Hard money lenders will offer short-term loans over six months and up to two years, which are backed by real estate. This will serve your purpose if you are looking to buy, renovate and sell the property. This will also come in handy for the quick expenses you'll have, like repairs and renovations. However, hard money lenders may only offer you up to 70% of the property value.
- House-flipping investors will also provide you with the funding required to purchase a house and flip it. However, since you're not bringing the funds, you will have to bring in the right contacts or deals to make the partnership work.
- Seller financing is when you buy a property financed by the seller. In other words, you agree to pay the owed sum to them over a period of time. The seller may be willing to take care of the renovation costs as well. Later, when you sell the property, you can pay

any outstanding costs to the seller, as well as what they have paid for the repairs, and still make a profit.

- Crowdfunding is a method whereby several small investors will help you with your purchase and the costs of renovating a property. Later, when you sell it, their money will be repaid from the proceeds.
- Live-in flipping is when you buy a property, live there, and get the renovations and repairs done. The advantage of this is that you may be eligible for loans from the U.S. Department of Veteran Affairs (VA) or the U.S. Department of Agriculture (USDA) at lower interest rates to cover the costs. These loans are for primary residences, thus, not suitable if you are considering flipping a property for rental.
  Additionally, there may be parts of the repair that you can undertake yourself and, thus, save money there as well.

3. **Buy and hold** is when you buy a property and hold on to it for a long time so you can ride the short-term market loss and then sell for a profit when property values eventually surge. There are several ways in which you can make an income on the property – one is by renting it out until you get the desired market value to sell the property.

- Vacation rentals allow you to rent your property out to vacationers and make a passive income. Whenever you want to, you can also use the property for your own living.
- Single-family tenants are safer than vacationers, as they tend to be long-term tenants, and the owner needs to interact with just one tenancy.

- Turnkey real estate is investing in ready-to-move properties which are managed by a company. The buyer can invest and then just wait for the income as tenants are found and managed by the company. The additional work, repair, and all other aspects will be handled by the company agents, and the fees will be deducted from the rental income.
- Investing in multi-family buildings will provide you with higher rental incomes as several families stay in multiple housing units within the same building. However, the cost of running such a setup is also higher.
- A commercial lease is when you buy a property and rent it out for commercial or business activities. Such leases have more complicated rental agreements and maintenance issues and must be approached with care.

4. **Real Estate Investment Trust (REIT)** works via companies that own income-producing properties like hotels, malls, restaurants, rental apartments, etc. Investors can buy, invest in, and sell REITs just as they do with stocks. This is easier on investors who don't want to be involved in the hassle of actually buying or selling property. It is an excellent method of diversifying your asset base and, over a long period, gives good returns owing to capital appreciation and steady dividend income. Here are some facts about purchasing and maintaining REITs:

- Just like any other public stock, REITs listed on the stock exchange can be purchased by an investor.
- REIT mutual funds or exchange-traded funds also offer shares to the investor who can purchase them.

- Many retirement investment plans, including the 401(k), invest in REITs to grow the principal. REITs are highly recommended by financial advisors as a means of providing high returns over an extended period.
- Normally a 5-15% allocation of your income in REIT from early career to retirement is advised by experts. Financial advisors will usually ask you to invest closer to 15% at the beginning of your career and slow the REIT allocation to about 7% of your income as you approach retirement.
- The REIT Directory provides a list of companies that trade in REITs. This list can be sorted according to performance, listing status, and sector.

I have broadly mentioned the ways in which real estate can help diversify your investment portfolio and how investing earlier rather than later can make all the difference.

Regardless of the assets you choose to invest in, one of the major concepts that any investor should understand is compound interest. We will now briefly examine how compound interest can help you effortlessly grow your money.

Growing Your Wealth Through Compound Interest

First things first. As touched on earlier, there are two ways of calculating interest.

Simple interest is when the interest you earn is only on your initial investment or the principal sum. For instance, suppose you invest $1,000 at an 8% yearly interest rate. Every year, you will earn an interest amount of $80. This means that in the first year, you will have a total of $1,080 in your account. In the second year, this figure will become $1,160, and so on.

Compound interest is when you earn interest on the principal and the interest earned. In the same example as above, if the interest is 8% compounded every year, you will earn $1,080 at the end of the first year. However, in the second year, the interest will be 8% of $1,080, not of $1,000. Thus, the interest after the second year will be $86.40, and the total sum will now be $1,166.40.

$6.40 looks like a minimal difference. However, on larger sums and over a long period of time, compound interest will give a much higher return than simple interest. Below is a comparison table between simple interest vs. compound interest with a $1,000 principle starting and a 5% interest rate compounded yearly over 10 years.

Interest rate =	5%	
	Simple Interest Earned	Compound Interest Earned
Initial Deposit	$1,000.00	$1,000.00
Year 1	$50.00	$50.00
2	$50.00	$55.00
3	$50.00	$55.25
4	$50.00	$58.01
5	$50.00	$60.91
6	$50.00	$63.96
7	$50.00	$67.16
8	$50.00	$70.51
9	$50.00	$74.04
10	$50.00	$77.74

Here are some things to understand about compound interest and the methods of investing to earn the maximum on compound interest:

1. Compound interest, as evident from the example above, works only if the investment happens over a long period of time. Over a year or two, the difference between simple interest and compound interest will be negligible. Over a decade or two, the difference will be significant.
2. When putting your money in a bank, check out your options and consider a high-yield savings account or certificate of deposits.
3. If you invest in shares, the dividends you earn can be re-invested. This means you will earn dividends on dividends, which is, in essence, compound interest.

Now we have looked at compound interest and how you can multiply money with time, let us look at how you can save your first $100,000.

Saving Your First $100,000

Reaching the target of $100,000 at the beginning is the hardest. Once you hit it, it is just a matter of continue investing wisely so you can grow your wealth even more.

The following table provides an estimate of how soon you can reach the target amount of $100,000 if you save between $100 and $1,000 monthly at the rates given.

Monthly amount deposited	Number of years to achieve target at rate of interest annually 5%	Number of years to achieve target at rate of interest annually 6%	Number of years to achieve target at rate of interest annually 7%	Number of years to achieve target at rate of interest annually 8%
100	33	30.5	27.5	25.5
250	20	18.5	17.5	16.5
500	12.5	11.5	11	10.7
750	8.8	8.5	8.3	7.9
1000	6.9	6.7	6.6	6.4

Note: I have used monthly compounded interest for the above chart.

Using the table above, you can see how compound interest can help you make your first $100,000, depending on the amount you can save monthly.

Key Takeaway

This section covers one of the ways you can invest your money beyond stocks and bonds. Investing in real estate can help you build wealth and increase your net worth over time. I hope you find the magic of compound interest as fascinating as I do and see a path forward of how this can help you hack your way to your first $100,000.

Let us now take a minute to reflect on how you have gotten this far. We've covered budgeting, saving money, clearing your debt, maintaining a good credit score, preparing for retirement, and investing wisely. All of these will stand you in good stead to do the best for yourself and your family. Now you arrive at a really important part of the book. How do we discuss money with family? Often regarded as taboo, talking about money is generally considered impolite or not in good taste. However, the next section will bust at least a few of these myths and give you an idea of how we can talk about money in the best interests of everyone involved.

8

MONEY TALKS

WE NEED TO BREAK THE MONEY TABOO

Money is only a tool. It will take you wherever you wish, but it will not replace you as the driver.

AYN RAND

When I was young, personal finance was a subject that was seldom discussed in my family. On the rare occasions that money was brought up in a conversation, it was often in a negative context, such as "it's difficult to make money" or "we don't have enough". I was warned at a young age not to ask questions like "What's someone's salary?" or while splitting bills, not to ask outright, "How much do I owe you?" I also heard my family discussing our relatives' debts behind their backs, but nobody would ever ask them upfront about how it happened or how they planned to get out of it. The list of questions not to ask about money was endless. The net effect was that I learned to internalize money as being this essential but inherently dirty commodity that must not be named aloud.

However, as I grew older, I found fault with this theory. I don't mean that I pry into and question the lives of people who gets into financial difficulties. But I often did try to find out more details of what led to their predicament and tried to help them out with suggestions and ideas that I had found through my own ample reading on finances. I frequent finance forums and online groups, reading about people's financial journeys and how they resolve their sticky money situations. Many of these people were really open to suggestions and were not in the least bit embarrassed to share their stories with me and others about how they had made a mistake, been tricked by fancy agents, or had simply made bad choices because they didn't know better. Another sad reality is that many of these people didn't even make "mistakes". They did what society tells them to do—go to college and get a good job. They took out loans for their degrees, but when they graduated, they did not land a job that pay enough to live comfortably and pay off debts. I, for my part, gained valuable insight into improving my own personal finance and the common mistakes to avoid when budgeting, saving, and investing. As they say, there's only so much that books can teach you; our greatest life lessons often come from our experiences. Vicariously, I learned a lot from others, which has helped me immensely on my own financial journey.

This chapter will give you insights into how money can be discussed with friends and family and will bust the myth that talking about money is taboo. It is, in my opinion, imperative to talk about money with the people you trust, who can provide a valuable perspective on personal finance. Just as one discusses art, architecture, music, work, food, or any other subject for that matter, money is a vital tool of human civilization. Talking about it also gives one the opportunity to connect with others, learn about your market value for your skill sets, and generally help you feel less lonely on your financial journey. Because money is a tool to help us achieve financial freedom and it plays a big role in many people's lives, it becomes essential that we learn to be comfortable and open to talk about money with less guilt and shame.

Discussing Money With Friends

One of the biggest reasons that we fear conversations around money is because it makes us feel vulnerable. We assume that others could be deriding our choices or that we may feel inferior in a society that equates success to one's net worth. However, this is exactly why we should talk more about it. In fact, listening to people who have made the right choices when it comes to personal finance can do wonders in improving yours. And imagine if it's a close and trustworthy friend – the aid you can receive in terms of borrowed experience. So let us look at how this could work in your favor.

Starting the Conversation

Without realizing it, a lot of the conversations we have with friends are already centered around finances. They might be related to purchasing a new phone, going out to restaurants, just having bought a car, and so on. One of the best methods to start a conversation about money is to share your personal worries or anxieties about it. For instance, tell your friends that you would love to opt for a certain lifestyle choice but just can't afford it at the moment. Or you could say that you have recently started saving but just can't figure out how to do it and also meet your expenses. When you open up about your fears, you will see that others naturally open up with suggestions or problems that they themselves have faced in the past and subsequently overcome.

Financial Fences

It is quite normal for friends to want to hang out together and meet at different places. This can become embarrassing when your friends keep suggesting places that are out of your current budget. Many youngsters feel the need to keep up with their peers, and they make some of the worst financial decisions in their early working life. An easy way out of this is to say upfront that the place suggested is a little out of your budget. You can contextualize this in terms of the recent budgeting or savings you are undertaking. You can then offer an alternative that fits into your budget. True friends will go out of their way to accommodate you. And if they don't? Perhaps you are better off without friends who regularly disregard your financial circumstances.

This rule is also applicable in reverse. If you are aware that your friends earn less than you, you should give them the choice of where they would like to meet. You cannot insist they meet you in a fancy or expensive joint too far out of their budget.

Friends Are Resources

Who said that you could learn things only within the confines of a classroom or from a book or the internet? Your friends can give you insights about so many aspects of life that you are unacquainted with, just as you can fill them in on some things they're not sure of. Financial literacy can be gleaned from friends who share some of the same goals as you. For instance, people who are serious about earning and saving, meeting their financial obligations, and aiming for financial growth can certainly illuminate your path with the dos and don'ts of investing. Talking to such people will point you in the direction of new ideas, resources, and goals for financial stability. You can also gain some foresight into the common pitfalls of investing and things to watch out for in order to make the right financial choices.

Remember that all learning is a two-way street. If you learn something from someone, be sure to pass on that knowledge to someone else who may benefit from it. Don't try to go on your personal finance journey alone. You can save yourself the headaches by learning from someone else's experience.

Set Goals Together

Remember how peer study helped you? And do you remember how group workouts in the gym enhanced your enthusiasm to remain fit? Well, the same applies to saving and investing. Having an accountability partner to set common goals and work towards them is one of the best ways to stay psychologically and motivationally on your target line. If you ever feel like slacking, your friend will pull you up, and vice versa. There is nothing like encouragement from trusted friends to spur you in the right direction. When one of you touches milestones, you can even have small celebrations or parties. There are also online forums and platforms where you can set financial goals and work towards them while staying incognito.

Learn, Don't Compare

As in every good game, healthy competition (especially with yourself) is a great way to improve yourself and raise the bar. However, comparing yourself with others can only bring misery. Let's face it – all of us are different. Our goals are different, and so are our priorities. Somebody may have saved more than you, but you might have cleared your outstanding debts sooner than them. The positive aspect of talking about finance is that you can always learn something new. There is always a better way to achieve a target – perhaps a shorter or simpler way? The chief aim of talking about money is to learn, and the minute this is replaced with the baser aim of outdoing or outwitting others, you have already failed.

Be Non-Judgmental

As in all other aspects of life, you never know what another has gone through in terms of their relationships, experiences, and background. While sharing and learning from experiences are essential, avoid judging a person's character based solely on their financial choices. Remember that good people can make terrible money mistakes, and personal finance is personal. You can lend them an ear and give them moral support. Likewise, when you make wrong decisions (which is sometimes a part of the learning curve), share these with people who can give you adequate psychological support to see you through it.

Discussing Money with Family

Just as with trusted friends, one can also be open about different aspects of finances with their family. This is especially so when parents are often children's first example of financial management. As teens, it is important for children to take an active interest in how different expenses of the household are met, who pays the bills, what each statement looks like, and how much it is likely to come to every month, etc. As one grows up, it is good to learn about the significant debts, loans, or liabilities that have been incurred by the family as well. This will enable youths to be prepared to a certain degree to take on responsibilities of their own. Let us look at some specific ways to partake in the money conversation with family:

1. **Get comfortable being uncomfortable.**
Talking about money can be difficult. Ensure you discuss various aspects of money management and not just the ones that are easiest to handle. When you don't understand something, follow up with specific questions, and try to learn as much about the subject as possible. Your parents have years of wisdom in handling finances, so they will naturally have many stories on how to and how not to do something. Listen, and mentally jot down all they say. Ask your parents about challenging subjects like how they negotiated their salary, how prepared they are to meet their retirement, possible medical costs, and how much aid you can expect towards meeting other important goals in your life, like saving for your first car or paying for college. Every family is different, and the answers to these questions will vary. If your family is not well-versed in financial literacy, you may seek help from other sources. Given that most people have access to the internet these days, there are several free online personal finance courses that can provide you with pillars for financial success, such as Udemy, Coursera, and Advanced Learning Interactive Systems Online (Alison). You may even join personal finance Facebook groups to connect with like-minded people.

2. **Respect your family members' choices.** It is acceptable to voice your opinions and suggestions regarding the household's finances. But remember that ultimately, it is your parent's house, and likely they will have the final say. You can present a logical argument for or against a particular way of doing things; however, you must also be reasonable in listening to their side of the story. Similarly, do not

force your parents into choices they are not comfortable with. For instance, how much college need-based aid you would be qualified for depends on your family's financial situation. Some students don't get assistance from their families to pay for college. A few may have been financially independent from their parents since they turned 18, and they have difficulty filing Free Application for Federal Student Aid (FAFSA) because their parents would not want to share with them their tax information. In these cases, you can't force your parents to do what they don't want to do, so you will have to file as independent. Another example I see with older adults is when they want their parents to move in with them or move to an assisted living home as they age; however, their parents may want to remain independent despite their struggles with daily tasks. The conversations you have with your parents must take into consideration their feelings and their want for privacy.

3. **Be patient.** Progress cannot be wrought in a day, nor will all conversations about money be covered in a single sitting. You may have to plan such conversations over a period of time so that everyone involved is given the opportunity to mull an idea over. It will take time and energy to foster open communication. Most importantly, there must be honesty on both sides. When there is a difference in opinion, both parties must be willing to listen to the other side and agree to disagree. As with any discussion, care must be taken not to hurt anyone personally.

Families who have had discussions about money claim they feel a greater sense of peace and preparedness for all financial problems that may befall them. I would go one step further and say that families who can discuss money and not fall apart over it will forge a really strong bond.

Discussing Estate Planning

This section will look at one particular topic which becomes contentious even in the best of families: estate planning. Simply put, estate planning is about how ancestral or family land or property will be divided up between its legal heirs. Though it sounds straightforward, often it is anything but. As a youngster, you may wonder, "Why worry about something that is still many years away?" Death is never a pleasant subject to broach; however, estate planning is best done earlier rather than later. It is always good to have the essential papers and documents of the estate in place and accessible to all the near and dear family you trust, and to whom you plan to will it. I will come to the papers and documents that must be kept ready in a little while.

More difficult than this first step is how you discuss this subject with your spouse or other family members so they know how to act and are sure of your intentions in case of your untimely demise.

The timing of the conversation must be carefully planned so you don't upset or ruffle people unnecessarily. A crisis situation may not be the ideal time to discuss such a thing, even though you might find it important to discuss it. However, when people are emotional or under stress, they may not be very receptive to your opinions or suggestions.

Though your intentions may be impeccable, your family may react in ways other than what you imagine. Remember, not everyone likes being reminded of the loss of a dear one. Thus, it is imperative to have an adequate introduction to the topic. Tell them why you are about to discuss your plans with them so your decisions will not catch them off guard.

When discussing something as financially important as estate planning, ensure that all parties with a stake in it are present. This will ensure that nobody is riled about being left out or not being kept in the loop. It will also show that you are not taking any sides and that your decisions are impartial and in the best interest of the family and the legalities of the estate.

There may be several difficulties while discussing this issue, so it is necessary to remain cool and calm while talking. It is best if you have already enlisted the help of an estate attorney or some other impartial consultant to help you draw up a plan. You must choose an able executor of your will from among your family members or someone you deeply trust. It is helpful to have a third-party present at family meetings, someone related to the estate. Do not give in to emotions – think and rethink before you make up your mind about any point.

If family members ask you challenging questions, you can have an attorney draft answers for them. Experts will already have a clear idea about the questions that may be thrown at you, so they can step in to ensure that it doesn't turn into a battle-ground of sorts.

Planning an estate can be a lot of work, and it helps if you stay as organized and methodical as possible. Be ready with the documents you may need in a separate file. These include:

1. **Power of attorney.** This will enable a trusted family member of your choice to make financial decisions on your behalf if anything should happen to you. Depending on the capacity you grant them, they will be able to withdraw money or represent you to make a financial deal, etc.

2. **Living will or a health care proxy.** A living will is your decision regarding the kind of medical care and treatment you would want if you were to meet with an incapacitating accident. Decisions about whether to be put on a ventilator, the kind of food and nutrition you would like, and so on can all be planned by you. A health care proxy is the appointment of a person who will make the above decisions in your place. Your health care proxy and the person you grant power of attorney can be the same or two different individuals.

3. **Will.** This is the legal document in which you set forth how your assets are to be divided and whom you appoint as the executor of the will to ensure your instructions are carried out. Without a will, the state will decide how your estate and property will be distributed.

4. **Revocable trust.** This is a written document of how you want your assets or estate handled in your lifetime and after you die. This is not a mandatory document, but it will help you plan ahead and hold your assets in the best interests of the beneficiaries. A revocable trust can be revoked at any time by its creator, which is you.

Finally, it is essential to understand that you are at liberty to change your mind. Things may come up which may change your perspective and outlook with respect to the planning of your estate. Consequently, new additions, deletions, or modifications may be necessary for your estate planning. Whatever the case may be, it is essential to keep the lines of communication open and to discuss the changes with everyone who holds a stake in your plans.

I have written this chapter from the assumption that many of you are just starting your financial journey. Many of you may feel like an estate plan isn't necessary because you don't have many assets yet. This couldn't be further from the truth. Even if you don't own a ton of assets, you still need an estate plan. An estate plan helps your estate avoid probate, which is a lengthy court proceeding to oversee the distribution of your estate. When you don't have an estate plan, it will be up to the state to decide how your estate is distributed. This may result in your assets not going to the beneficiaries you intended. Your estate includes personal property, life insurance, retirement accounts, etc. Additionally, in the instances where your health drastically declines, a proper estate plan will allow you to convey to your family your wishes for future medical care and relieve them from the burden of making an extremely difficult medical decision on your behalf. The cost of estate planning can vary depending on the complexity of your estate and the rate structures of your attorney. The cost can start around $1,500 and runs up to $3,000 or more. My best money hack for estate planning is to opt for the legal plan via your employer if available. You can save yourself several thousand dollars by utilizing your company's legal benefits for estate planning.

Now, it may very well be that you are also on the receiving side of inheritance. Remember that if you are expecting an inheritance and have yet to receive it, don't assume you will get it. The person owning the assets may change their mind if their circumstances change. However, if you do receive an inheritance, depending on what kind of asset it is, you will need to work with the executor of the estate to transfer the asset to your name. You may also consider seeking professional advice if you are not comfortable making the financial decision on your own. If disputes arise during the planning of the estate or when the estate is executed, it is important to remember the larger picture – that family is a powerful bond and that one must not lose sight of what's important over more minor considerations like money. Learn to manage your expectation. Most disputes happen when an expectation of receiving an inheritance is not met. I'll repeat this again: don't include an inheritance in your financial plan until it is in your name. If the dispute continues, the family can get a mediator involved to serve as a neutral third party helping to work out the differences.

Key Takeaway

When you plan your finances, you are planning not just for yourself but for your loved ones too. Just as you make your best decisions about retirement, it is essential to go one step further to plan whatever you can for when you're gone. This will ensure that your grieving family will not be under more stress than they ought to be. In such planning, it makes sense to consult an estate agent, legal professional, or an impartial third party who can advise the best course of action. This will also ensure that you are not so emotionally stressed that you make errors of judgment or poor decisions. Experts will quickly spot difficulties or problems in your plans and warn you about how they can be surmounted. Seek legal assistance to create a comprehensive living trust, and make sure to have an open honest discussion regarding your decisions with all family members. This will prevent miscommunication or disagreement among your family when the time comes to execute your estate. Finally, regardless of others' opinions, plan your estate in the way that feels right for you. Your estate plan is ultimately your decision.

CONCLUSION

There is a fountain of youth: it is your mind, your talents, the creativity you bring to your life and the lives of people you love. When you learn to tap this source, you will truly have defeated age.

SOPHIA LOREN

Being young is an exhilarating time of life. You have so much on your side: energy, a sense of never-ending optimism, and a whole life to look forward to. Financially speaking, most of you will have just gotten into stable jobs and will be looking at building up your life, one step at a time. There are so many new things to discover – new relationships, a fresh career, and the promise of success – things that would spur anybody to live life to the fullest. Some say that the young are rash, that they don't have a sense of purpose, and they live for the present without any care for the future, but I beg to differ. The young are very wise. With a nudge in the right direction, the potential that youth wield is enormous. It is perhaps true that they lack in the experience department, but they can more than make up for it if they are willing to learn the right financial skills at the right time.

As I see it, life boils down to just that – timing. As a society rooted in the present, we tend to unthinkingly use the term *carpe diem* as a mantra that ought to solve all our problems. We believe that finding happiness is linked to the present. And though I think this is partly true, I would also argue that real happiness comes from securing one's future as well. *Carpe diem* gets one thing right at any rate – the fleeting transience of life. When we recognize life's brevity, we put in measures to do our bit to safeguard our and our loved ones' future. I am convinced that therein lies real happiness and true peace. I hope this book has given you the keys to securing your future with the resources at your disposal. All it takes is a little learning, a little effort, some planning, and a lot of execution.

To quickly recap, things that are in your power to do now are:

1. Budget
2. Save
3. Stay free from bad debts
4. Build a credit score
5. Plan your retirement
6. Ensure everything you hold dear
7. Invest and grow
8. Talk money

I don't believe that anything we achieve in life is through sheer luck. It is mostly a combination of luck, a little work, and lots of fortitude.

There is a story I once read: a farmer had three lazy sons who would hardly do their part in tending to the fields. They lay about day after day, worrying about nothing and whiling away their time in frivolous pursuits. The lion's share of the work was always done by the old man. He was worried about them, wondering what would befall them after his time. As he realized his time was drawing near, he told them, "I have buried a large treasure in our fields for you to live off after my time." The lazy sons were surprised and pleased that they had this bounty at their disposal. They wanted to hear the details, to which the old man replied, "It was a very long time ago, and I have forgotten the exact location now. But you will find it; just keep searching." And as much as they pestered him, this was all he would reveal to them.

After their father's death, the sons started digging the fields to search for this treasure. They dug frenetically. They were in a hurry to find the treasure. After days of digging, however, they started to wonder. Had the old man played some colossal joke on them? Was he raving mad to have led them on this wild goose chase? Or was he exacting some form of revenge from sons who had never really been of any help to him? The perplexed sons were sitting around thinking about what to do when an old, wise sage came their way. He told them that as they had dug up so much of the earth anyway, they might as well plant the seeds for the coming harvest. The sons decided to do that.

That year the harvest was plentiful, and they made a significant profit selling the crops. From the profits, they bought a tractor which made their lives a little easier in the coming year. The year after that, they were able to invest in a sprinkler. Soon the fields were supported by hands who were paid to work on them, and a farm was established right next to them. At this point, the sons diversified their interests and started selling various products. They had become rich and prosperous.

As their time was coming to an end, they happened to meet the same sage. They hailed him and told him how he had turned their lives around. The sage replied with a twinkle in his eyes, "No, not I. It is your father who realized the treasure that he had left you. You were just too lazy to see it. But because you dug for the 'treasure,' you have gained it now." The sons were stunned, realizing what their father had done for them. They had often wondered whether it was senility or bitterness that had made their father lie to them about a non-existent treasure. But now they saw that the treasure was the land they had owned since the beginning. All it required was some work.

I love this story because it is our story as well. When we crib that we are fated to have nothing in life, more often than not, there is an answer right in front of us. Barring severe hardships or a traumatic past, we are all given the same chances to work, invest, and reap the benefits of our hard work. However, when immediate concerns distract us, we often lose this tenuous grip over what could have been a comfortable future. With a little effort and the proper guidance, all of us have it in us to become financially stable and secure.

Like the sons who finally found their treasure, I hope you do too, dear reader!

LEAVE A REVIEW AND HELP OTHER READERS START THEIR PERSONAL FINANCE JOURNEY!

If you find this book helpful in any way, I would appreciate a short review of the book. As a self-published author, I do read every review. Thank you for your kind support of my book!

May 2023 be the year you find your financial happy place!

Scan the QR code below for the Amazon review page.

CONNECT WITH THE AUTHOR

Thank you so much for reading this book and supporting my work. Over a decade ago, I wrote on my bucket list that I wanted to publish a book. It's so surreal to see this book comes to life after several months. I hope you find the information in this book beneficial in some ways. If you want to connect with me and talk about all things personal finance, please email me at phuang.22@outlook.com. I am no financial expert—just a regular person with an interest in personal finance, so please don't hesitate to reach out. I learned many things that helped kickstart my financial journey because I got curious and decided to no longer see money as a taboo topic. I wouldn't have my first credit card or negotiate my first salary if I didn't learn to be comfortable talking about money with others. If you don't have anyone you can chat with about money, I hope I can be that person. Richard Stallman said, "*Sharing knowledge is the most fundamental act of friendship. Because it is a way, you can give something without losing something.*" I've been very blessed to have many great friends in my life, and I would love to pass on this blessing to others.

Thank you again for your time and for picking up this book. Please take a minute to leave a review on Amazon or any platform you get this book. This would mean the world to me. I read every review and welcome any feedback. I wish you all the best in your financial journey. Cheers!

BIBLIOGRAPHY

10 tips on budgeting for teens in 2022. (2022, June 14). Teen Financial Freedom. Retrieved September 15, 2022, from https://teenfinancialfree dom.com/10-tips-on-budgeting-for-teens/

30 ways to cut your monthly expenses. (2017, November 6). Lifehack. Retrieved September 15, 2022, from https://www.lifehack.org/articles/money/30-ways-cut-your-monthly-expenses.html

Agadoni, L. (2021, November 22). *How young people can get started in real estate investing.* The Motley Fool. Retrieved September 15, 2022, from https://www.fool.com/investing/2021/11/22/how-young-people-can-get-started-in-real-estate-in/

Albaum, M. (2021, September 27). *Why you should invest in real estate young (and how to do it).* Learn Real Estate Investing. Retrieved September 15, 2022, from https://learn.roofstock.com/blog/investing-in-real-estate-young

Ballentine, C. (2021, December 8). *When can I retire? Gen Z wants to stop working before 55, Goldman Sachs says.* Bloomberg.com. Retrieved September 15, 2022, from https://www.bloomberg.com/news/articles/2021-12-08/when-can-i-retire-gen-z-wants-to-stop-working-before-55-gold man-sachs-says

Beginner's Guide to Refinancing Your Student Loans. (n.d.). ISL Education Lending. Retrieved September 15, 2022, from https://www.iowastudent loan.org/articles/college/beginners-guide-to-refinancing.aspx

Bell, A. (2022, July 8). *6 reasons why you need a budget.* Investopedia. Retrieved September 15, 2022, from https://www.investopedia.com/financial-edge/1109/6-reasons-why-you-need-a-budget.aspx

Bieber, C. (2018, July 9). *How long will it take you to save your first $100,000?.* The Motley Fool. Retrieved September 15, 2022, from https://www.fool.com/investing/2018/07/09/how-long-will-it-take-you-to-save-your-first-10000.aspx

Catmull, J. (2022, June 22). *4 biggest financial hurdles for gen Z that no one else has faced.* GOBankingRates. Retrieved September 15, 2022, from https://www.gobankingrates.com/money/financial-planning/4-biggest-financial-hurdles-for-gen-z-that-no-one-else-has-faced/

Compound interest calculator. (n.d.). Compound Interest Calculator | Investor.-gov. Retrieved September 13, 2022, from https://www.investor.gov/finan cial-tools-calculators/calculators/compound-interest-calculator

Daly, L. (2022, February 8). *How to pay off debt: The ascent.* The Motley Fool.

Retrieved September 15, 2022, from https://www.fool.com/the-ascent/personal-finance/how-to-pay-off-debt/

Daugherty, G. (2022, March 29). *Can teenagers invest in Roth IRAs?* Investopedia. Retrieved September 15, 2022, from https://www.investopedia.com/can-teenagers-invest-in-roth-iras-4770663

Davis, G. B. (n.d.). *10 ways to avoid lifestyle inflation – spending less when you earn more.* Money Crashers. Retrieved September 15, 2022, from https://www.moneycrashers.com/ways-avoid-lifestyle-inflation/

Dunlap, T. (2019, May 30). *I'm 24 and on track to save $100,000 by next year- here are my money-saving tips.* CNBC. Retrieved September 15, 2022, from https://www.cnbc.com/2019/05/28/im-24-and-on-track-to-save-100000-next-year-here-are-my-money-saving-tips.html

Eastman, D. (2022, June 28). *Buy-and-hold investing: Real estate investing.* Kiavi. Retrieved September 15, 2022, from https://www.kiavi.com/blog/buy-and-hold-real-estate-investing

Elkins, K. (2017, May 29). *10 small things to give up if you want to save more money.* CNBC. Retrieved September 15, 2022, from https://www.cnbc.com/2017/05/26/things-to-give-up-if-you-want-to-save-more-money.html

Fay, B. (2022, April 21). *Top 11 mistakes when trying to get out of debt quickly.* Debt.org. Retrieved September 15, 2022, from https://www.debt.org/advice/10-mistakes-getting-out-of-debt/

Ferreira, N. M. (2022, September 6). *11 best side Hustle Ideas to make an extra $1,000 a month.* Oberlo. Retrieved September 15, 2022, from https://www.oberlo.com/blog/side-hustle

Gjorgievska, L. (2022, May 1). *What is a 401k in Australia? the definitive guide.* Take a Tumble. Retrieved September 15, 2022, from https://takeatumble.com.au/guides/what-is-a-401k-in-australia/#:~:text=The%20equivalent%20of%20a%20401K,workers%20can%20use%20after%20retirement.

Gobler, E. (2022, April 18). *How to talk about money with your friends.* The Balance. Retrieved September 15, 2022, from https://www.thebalance.com/how-to-talk-about-money-with-your-friends-5209872

Greenthal, S. (2022, March 18). *Steps for young adults to open and maintain a 401(k).* The Balance. Retrieved September 15, 2022, from https://www.thebalance.com/opening-a-retirement-account-4155872

Hicks, C. (2022, November 6). *How to choose a financial advisor .* U.S. News. Retrieved September 15, 2022, from https://money.usnews.com/financial-advisors/articles/how-to-choose-a-financial-advisor

Hogan, P. (2017, September 15). *Roth IRA for Canadians and newcomers to Canada.* Phil Hogan, CPA, CA, CPA (CO). Retrieved September 15, 2022, from https://philhogan.com/roth-ira/

How credit works. (n.d.). The University of Oklahoma. Retrieved September 15, 2022, from https://www.ou.edu/moneycoach/financialeducation/cred-

it#:~:text=It's%20a%20financial%20commit-
ment%20to,safe%20to%20lend%20you%20money.

How to build an emergency fund [quick guide for 18-30 year olds]. (2022, July 7). Scholly. Retrieved September 15, 2022, from https://myscholly.com/how-to-build-an-emergency-fund/

How to invest in Real Estate Investment Trusts (REITs). (n.d.). Nareit. Retrieved September 15, 2022, from https://www.reit.com/investing/how-invest-reits

How to start house hacking when you're under 25. (2019, September 22). Young, Dumb, and NOT Broke?! Retrieved September 15, 2022, from https://youngdumbandnotbroke.com/house-hacking-when-youre-under-25/

How to start saving money: 8 money saving tips. (2022, February 25). Better Money Habits. Bank of America. Retrieved September 15, 2022, from https://bettermoneyhabits.bankofamerica.com/en/saving-budgeting/ways-to-save-money

How to talk to your family about planning your estate. (2017, June 20). ARAG . Retrieved September 15, 2022, from https://www.araglegal.com/member/learning-center/topics/planning-your-legacy/how-to-talk-to-family-about-planning-estate

Irby, L. (2022, June 1). *10 strategies for paying off your debt with no money.* The Balance. Retrieved September 15, 2022, from https://www.thebalance.com/how-to-pay-off-debt-when-you-re-broke-3875583

Jordan, A. (2020, November 18). *Explaining the benefits of a 401(k) to young adults entering the workforce.* Hudson Community Foundation. Retrieved September 15, 2022, from https://www.myhcf.org/blog-01/explaining-benefits-401k-young-adults-entering-workforce

Konish, L. (2019, February 11). *This is the real reason most Americans file for bankruptcy.* CNBC. Retrieved September 13, 2022, from https://www.cnbc.com/2019/02/11/this-is-the-real-reason-most-americans-file-for-bankruptcy.html

Lake, R. (2022, July 18). *How to improve your credit score fast.* Investopedia. Retrieved September 15, 2022, from https://www.investopedia.com/how-to-improve-your-credit-score-4590097

Marquit, M. (2022, January 16). *How to set savings goals: 6 tips.* Bankrate. Retrieved September 15, 2022, from https://www.bankrate.com/banking/savings/how-to-set-savings-goals/

Martel, J. (2022, July 6). *Roth IRAs for young adults: Moneyunder30.* Money Under 30. Retrieved September 15, 2022, from https://www.moneyunder30.com/roth-iras-for-young-adults#:~:text=While%20young%20people%20who%20are,or%2021%20in%20some%20states

Martin, E. (2017, September 22). *6 things to do in your 20s to be debt-free by 30.* CNBC. Retrieved September 15, 2022, from https://www.cnbc.com/2017/09/22/how-to-pay-off-loans-in-your-20s-and-be-debt-free-by-30.html

McMaken, L. (2022, May 27). *4 types of insurance policies and coverage you need*. Investopedia. Retrieved September 15, 2022, from https://www.investopedia.com/financial-edge/0212/4-types-of-insurance-everyone-needs.aspx

Merrill, T. (2022, August 25). *9 ways to flip houses with no money in 2022*. FortuneBuilders. Retrieved September 15, 2022, from https://www.fortunebuilders.com/how-to-flip-houses-with-no-money/

Mlc. (2021, July 9). *How to help grow your money through compound interest*. MLC. Retrieved September 15, 2022, from https://www.mlc.com.au/personal/blog/2020/02/how_to_help_growyou

Monthly budget spreadsheet for Young Adults. (2006). Wells Fargo. Retrieved September 15, 2022, from https://images.template.net/wp-content/uploads/2016/02/26071004/Monthly-Budget-Spreadsheet-for-Young-Adults-PDF-Free-Download.pdf

O'Brien, S. (2022, July 26). *THE STUDY SHOWS THAT Gen Z is stashing away 14% of income for retirement - more than older generations*. CNBC. Retrieved September 15, 2022, from https://www.cnbc.com/2022/07/26/gen-z-saving-14percent-of-income-for-retirement-more-than-other-generations.html

Palmer, K. (2014, August 20). *How to Talk Honestly About Money With Your Family*. U.S.News. Retrieved September 15, 2022, from https://money.usnews.com/money/personal-finance/articles/2014/08/20/how-to-talk-honestly-about-money-with-your-family

Paulus, N. (2022, August 15). *Becoming an investor in real estate rental properties*. MoneyGeek.com. Retrieved September 15, 2022, from https://www.moneygeek.com/mortgage/resources/rental-property-investing/

Plan your retirement income. (2015, February 4). GOV.UK. Retrieved September 15, 2022, from https://www.gov.uk/plan-retirement-income/your-pension-options

Retirement income. (n.d.). Moneysmart.gov.au. Retrieved September 15, 2022, from https://moneysmart.gov.au/retirement-income

Schreier, H. (2020, July 30). *Personal finance for young adults: Estate planning*. Forbes. Retrieved September 15, 2022, from https://www.forbes.com/sites/halseyschreier/2020/07/30/personal-finance-for-young-adults-estate-planning/?sh=6f62316e3a10

Sheffey, A. (2021, October 10). *Meet a 57-year-old dad with $104,000 in student debt for his son: 'it was my obligation to do the best I could for him'*. Business Insider. Retrieved September 1, 2022, from https://www.businessinsider.in/policy/economy/news/meet-a-57-year-old-dad-with-104000-in-student-debt-for-his-son-it-was-my-obligation-to-do-the-best-i-could-for-him/articleshow/86911711.cms

The shockingly simple math behind early retirement. (2012, January 13). Mr.

Money Mustache. Retrieved September 15, 2022, from https://www.mrmoneymustache.com/2012/01/13/the-shockingly-simple-math-behind-early-retirement/

Vishakha, R. M. (2021, October 12). *Why you should opt for Life Insurance at a young age.* Forbes. Retrieved September 15, 2022, from https://www.forbes.com/advisor/in/insurance/why-you-should-opt-for-life-insurance-at-a-young-age/

What is budgeting and why is it important?. (n.d.). My Money Coach. Retrieved September 15, 2022, from https://www.mymoneycoach.ca/budgeting/what-is-a-budget-planning-forecasting

What is credit and why is it important?. (n.d.). My Great Lakes. Retrieved September 15, 2022, from https://mygreatlakes.org/educate/knowledge-center/credit.html#:~:text=Credit%20is%20part%20of%20y-our,loans%20when%20you%20need%20them.

Yochim, D., & Coombes, A. (2021, November 29). *Roth vs. traditional IRA: Which is right for you?.* NerdWallet. Retrieved September 15, 2022, from https://www.nerdwallet.com/article/investing/roth-or-traditional-ira-account